To Mother for her 90th Birthday,

Ruth (Martin) Hawkins

7 March 2013.

That the

Generation to come

might know them . . . .

Psalm 78:6

Author Notes

My Dad suddenly dropped dead at an A's Baseball game in September 1984. He was 62 years old. It was very hard learning how to live without him. When he passed away, it was to be an experience that I have never been able to describe, endure, or express my feelings of what an incredible loss it still is. He was such a wonderful father, who had a special place for each of his children, we never felt neglected or envious of his feelings for one another. We shared him equally and totally. Although we have had to experience his death in our own individual ways, I did not realize that I had been predestined or led toward this particular direction all my life, as a so called family historian.

I was born in 1948 and grew up on a beautiful tree-lined street in Berkeley, California. My childhood and my life up to that time were idyllic as was that period for me. World War II was over, Eisenhower, a republican was president, and I was part of a generation now known as "Baby Boomers".

My father and mother came from Texas. My Dad had traveled to California while in the Navy, upon his discharge and after they got married; my parents made California their home. My younger sister and I grew up in a neighborhood with a mixture of nationalities as rich as any tapestry of colors. First and second generation Europeans; Asian, Mexican, South American and African American children were our childhood friends. We knew everyone on the block and beyond and they knew us. It was like the popular TV shows during that period; "Ozzie and Harriet", "Father Knows Best", and "Leave It to Beaver", except for one thing, none of those colors I just mentioned was present on the TV screen, except the Europeans. Although our images didn't appear in the popular TV shows, we were there in life.

My father took us on family vacations to visit our relatives in Texas and we visited other southern towns, as a child I was unaware of "Segregation" and "Separate but Equal" doctrines. I really didn't know about any of that until the 1960s, when I became painfully aware of what kind of world I really lived in. My parents did a great job of sheltering myself and my siblings from the real world.

What I learned about and had the opportunity was to meet my grandparents and great-grandmothers, aunts and uncles; cousins that I formed life-long relationships with. My mother is a wonderful story-teller and she would enthrall my sister, brother and I, with all the stories of her childhood and her mean step-fathers and stories about other family members. Some were very funny and some were very sad. There is not a family gathering today where someone does not recall a "character" or incident from one of my Mom's old stories.

My Dad was the family photographer; he recorded our childhood, family social gatherings, picnics and graduations, I inherited the job from him. I also became the recipient of family heirlooms given to me from older family members. My father's cousin gave me a collection of old family photographs that she had inherited from her mother that she passed to me shortly before she died.

Life interrupted my dreams of researching my father's family, temporarily; with immediate family, working and fulfilling another dream, operating my own bookstore. Owning my multicultural bookstore, further prepared me with the wealth of literary works of many great writers, multicultural and African American. I applied my knowledge of photography with my education in black and white photography darkroom techniques. I welcomed the collection I had inherited, to restore and preserve it for future generations. As I looked at the photos of family members that I did not know, I wanted to learn more about them. I began interviewing my remaining relatives and began writing as much information about the family members that I learned. I realized how fortunate I was to be able to get the information from my father's cousin so many years ago. I have found out information about my father's family that he would have been so pleased to know. I learned to keep him with me by finding his family.

My mother became interested in my researching my father's family and of course she wanted me to study her family. My mother's stories and other members of her family contributed their stories. The research that began years ago became the basis for this first book written about my family. To aid in my research, I have conducted interviews with many of our living relatives. Most were very eager to tell the story of our family as they knew it. I found that my mother wasn't the only one who enjoyed telling stories. Many of the stories helped me to locate some of the facts that I have uncovered. There were also members who chose not to contribute to this book; as a result there may be more information about some than others. Also, there may be more information simply because I may know or have actually known the subject or family member. I made every attempt to include everyone known to me, and others in the family who told me of those I didn't know. Although I have compiled this work as a book of memories and stories about our family, it is also a family history based on years of research conducted by me.

We are descendants of lumber mill or saw mill laborers; some were very skilled craftsmen and talented carpenters. The piney woods of East Texas, is where our people lived, worked, built their homes and raised their families. Some later generations left the place of their birth and migrated to other parts of the United States. But, basically our family did not have a desire to move, most are still living at or near the place of their birth. These are their stories.

Acknowledgments

I thank God and the Ancestors, without whom, none of this would be possible or necessary.

I am grateful for the encouragement that I have received to complete this work. My greatest supporter has always been my mother. She is the one who wanted me to complete this project from the beginning. I thank all my relatives that were able to offer insight into the lives of our ancestors and all the help I received along this journey. I thank my Aunt Ruby (Martin) for her back-up memory to my mother, and for finding the infamous Bible.

There are many in the genealogical community that I would like to thank; my special group in Solano County, I'm proud to have served as your 1st president, the African American Genealogical Society of Solano County, (AAGSSC), my members who acted as sounding boards and encouragement. I am also grateful for the information, genealogy workshops, and support offered by the African American Genealogical Society of Northern California, (AAGSNC), I am proud to be a member for the past six years.

There are many librarians who've offered their wealth of resources, information and the forums for my workshops. To my local libraries, Solano County Libraries; in Fairfield, Cordelia and Suisun, there's no place like home, thank you Serena Enger, Linda Williams, Peggy Yost, Nefertari Guice and Jim Silverman. I am especially grateful to Cindy McMullin, at the Kurth Memorial Library and all the folks at the Angelina County Genealogical Society in Texas. I couldn't have done my research without them. To my childhood mentor, Dr. Joel Fort, who continued to nurture my love of books, when I was young with access to his library and as I became an adult, with continued support when I opened by book store, his encouragement and cheering me on to this day.

I am grateful to the state of Texas for their historical resources: Kurth Memorial Library, The Clayton Historical Library, Houston; SMU Central University Libraries Texas; Texas State Historical Association, The Handbook of Texas Online and the newest resource, The Handbook of African-American Texas, I appreciate the records and historical resources in Texas.

To my family; again many of you, too numerous to mention, I needed and welcomed your support, my sister Brenda, my cousin Jody; I just want to thank you all. To my husband, Henry, thank you for your patience, for picking up the slack for us, when I was in another century. I am grateful for your love, encouragement and unselfish support.

In memory of my Dad, Warren G. Hawkins, Sr. (1923-1984), the reason I became interested and embarked on this genealogical journey.

Chapter 1

Marqurette to Joe

The story for this family begins in the early 1800s, that's approximately when Marqurette Smith was born in Texas. Although Texas was considered part of the southwest, Texas joined in with the Old South and in the process gave their state a definite Southern heritage. I mention this for a very good reason. The great majority of the new state's approximately 100,000 white inhabitants were natives of the South, who, as they settled in the eastern timberlands and south central plains, had built a life pretty much the same as they had in their home states of; Virginia, North Carolina, Georgia, Alabama, Louisiana and Arkansas. Texas was admitted to the union in 1845 as a slave state. Geographically a southwestern state with customs, traditions and the beliefs of the deep south.

Marqurette, an African American female, probably born into slavery in the early 1850s somewhere in San Jacinto County, which is in southeast Texas on the Trinity River, later parts of which would be known as Polk County. By 1857 Marqurette would be a young child, probably about three years old. It is not known who her parents were, you must understand that, she lived during a time when slaves were bought and sold, children were separated from their parents. What **is** known is that she survived the Civil War and slavery.

For Blacks in Texas, freedom did not come until "Juneteenth", June 19, 1865. Texas Blacks remained enslaved until the end of the Civil War. Few were able to run away and enlist in the Union Army, as Black men did in other parts of the South. For Texas, some slaves joined the confederacy along with their masters, and some in place of their masters.

Marqurette would have been about eleven years old when the war ended. Did she have to provide for herself, or maybe she was searching for her family? Did she know her parents? Did she have brothers and sisters? It is not known if she did, that was the usual predicament for most freed slaves after the war. She would be subjected to the reconstruction period which affected the politics, economics, education and social life for all Black Texans; reconstruction lasted about eight years. After reconstruction Marqurette had no equal protection under the law. Negroes faced a constant threat of violence. In Texas, between 1865 and 1868, 468 freedmen met violent deaths—90 percent at the hands of white men. In 1866 the "Black Codes" were created to continue legal discrimination. Black Codes kept freedmen from voting, holding political office, serving on juries, or testifying against whites in court. Marriage between the races was forbidden. The state required railroads to provide separate cars for Blacks, thus setting the pattern for segregation of all public facilities. Local customs followed the same general pattern in 1866, hotels and theaters segregated or refused admission to Black people. Whites killed Blacks for making a display of their freedom, for refusing to remove their hats when whites passed, for refusing to be whipped and many other indignities they could think of to humiliate, intimidate and harass people of color.

It was during this general social climate, in January 1869, Marqurette gave birth to a son, and she named him Joe. Margurette the mother of Joe, her last name, or maiden name is documented as Smith. This information was located on Joe's death certificate that also places her origins in San Jacinto County. Margurette was probably born in the mid 1800s, about 1850. This estimate is due to the ages of her children as documented on census reports.

The only other known relative for Joe is a sister, named Annie. This information was discovered during oral interviews with the grandchildren of Joe and Alice. Annie was said to have lived in Rayburn, Texas.

Chapter 2

Alice and Houston -Alice and Joe

Alice's mother's name was Hulda Odom, she was born in the state of Virginia, about 1841. Hulda was located on the US 1880 census listed as: head of household, Black, widowed and a farmer, living in Angelina County, in the town of Diboll. All of her children were listed as Mulatto.

It is not known how long she had lived in Texas. She may have been brought to Texas as a slave. Many slaves were brought to Texas from other southern states in anticipation of the dispute with the United States over the issue of slavery. It is not known if Hulda was brought to Texas as a slave or, possibly came as a free person of color, or may have been freed after coming to Texas.

Texas in 1880 was still trying to overcome the changes brought on by the Civil War. White Texans reluctantly accepted the end of slavery. Newspapers used the term "nigger", compared freedmen to apes and wrote news articles making "white" as everything pure and innocent and "black" as a substitute for wickedness and death. The ex-confederate majority constantly opposed the extension of social or political rights and equality to Blacks.

Hulda lived in Angelina County, possibly Ewing or Diboll. All of Hulda's children were born in Texas: Laura (1869); Alice (1875)*; William (1877). The place of birth for the children's father was listed as Texas also. This indicates that Hulda was at least in Texas by the time of her first child's birth, in 1869, four years after the end of the Civil War. Family oral history dictates that Alice was born in Ewing, Angelina County.

Notes: Alice's age varies from dob as 1874 to 1876, it's listed in the family Bible (1876), census reports (1875), her grave headstone and death certificate (1874), note that, prior to the 20th century most dates were approximate, dates of birth for African Americans were not always recorded for various reasons.

Ewing, Texas was on the Angelina and Neches River Railroad ten miles southeast of Lufkin in northeastern Angelina County. In 1920 it was the site of a hardwood lumber mill, active from 1920 to

1944. The old Ewing plantation had had the largest number of slaves in Angelina County at the time of the Civil War.

Diboll, Texas on US Highway 59, three miles north of the Neches River in southern Angelina County, was founded in 1894 when Thomas Lewis Latane Temple built a sawmill on the Houston, East and West Texas Railway (HE&WT R/R). Temple purchased the land from J.C. Diboll and built Southern Pine Lumber Company.

Houston Jackson was born in Texas about 1870, according to the US 1900 Census. He is listed as Black and his parents' origin is unknown. Houston was employed as a servant in the house of Mr. William Davis. Houston was 30 years old at the time, living in Lufkin, Angelina County, Texas. He is the father of Alice's two oldest children: Lottie May Jackson (dob 1891), and Houston Jackson 2nd (dob 1893), as recorded on Houston 2nd's death certificate. Alice was a young girl when she "married" *Houston Jackson 1st. Estimates place Alice's age at about 16 years old at the time of birth of her first child, Lottie May.

Based on research gathered so far, Alice (Odom) Smith, was born somewhere in Angelina County, Texas. Alice's early life was spent in Ewing and eventually Diboll, Texas. Research places Alice in Diboll by the time she meets Joe Smith. Joe grew up during the reconstruction period, the time after the Civil War when Blacks were set free and for a brief period had equal rights and privileges under the law. Research had not uncovered any specific information about Joe's early life. Ruth and Ruby Martin describe their grandfather as being called Papa or Grandpa, "he had big, beautiful eyes and he was a big, tall, dark, handsome man." Grandma was this "tiny, barely four-foot tall, woman with very light skin, many who saw her would think she was white".

They begin their lives in Angelina County, Joe's work as a sawmill laborer will take them to many towns in Angelina and Polk Counties. For reasons known only to him, and possible regional influences, Joe would not be a farmer or work in agricultural labor; he became a skilled laborer in the lumber industry. Railroad construction brought several thousand Negroes to Texas in the 1870s. Several large lumber mills were established along the Houston East and West Texas Railway (HE&WT R/R). Palmetto Lumber Company was established in San Jacinto County between 1869 and 1874. In East Texas Black lumber workers formed 42 percent of the 6,350 men employed by that industry in 1890. What was life like for Alice and Joe during this period, the late 1860s to 1900s? In 1898, the average cost of a home was $4,000.00, a loaf of bread cost $.03

(cents), milk was $.26 (cents) a gallon, the average income for a worker was $630.00 per year for a white worker, for a Black worker the average income based on saw mill wages is $260.00 per year.

Joe and Alice filed for a marriage certificate 20 January 1898, in Polk County. Joe was 29 years old and Alice was twenty-two. When Joe meets Alice, she already has two children; Lottie May and Houston 2nd. They would add ten more by the time of the last child's birth in 1916. The total number of children with names and dates of birth would be discovered in a family Bible belonging to Joe and Alice's daughter Willie Ruth, which helped greatly in the research of our family.

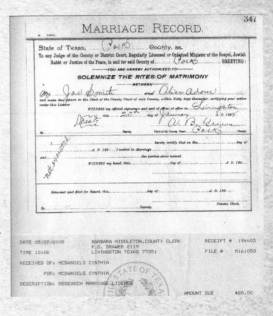

By 1900 Joe and Alice were living and working in Diboll, Texas. Diboll was a typical company town, owned by Southern Pine Lumber Company. Many of its homes, built from lumber produced by the Southern Pine Mills, were owned by the lumber company and rented to employees. Sawmill towns were a separate part of all the communities surrounding them. Sawmill towns were usually built near or because of the railroad. In the lumber industry, the two worked together. The towns were their own little world, apart from regular society. They were designed to keep the workers accessible to the workings of the mill and nothing else. Many of them paid workers with company "script", this script was payable only to the sawmill town's commissaries; clothing and food suppliers. Joe and Alice lived in the part of town designated for Blacks. This was called "the quarters", they were equipped with some of the same conveniences as the whites. They had their churches, pool hall, barber shop, hotel (boarding home for Blacks), and cemetery. The accommodations for Blacks were of course on a much smaller, lower quality scale. Blacks had to stay on their side of town. They had their own school, usually a one room shack and as they did nearly everywhere else, Black students used old, worn-out textbooks throw out by the white institutions.

The average Black sawmill worker was a hard drinking, gambling, fighting man, working long hours, of most of the hardest work required at a sawmill. Some men attended church on Sunday with their families, at some point Joe did, after learning to read. Daughter Willie taught him how to read from the Bible. Men like Joe were dedicated to the lumber industry, rarely would a sawmill worker become a farmer or venture into another vocation.

According to the US 1900 census dated 16 June 1900, Joe is listed with wife, Alice; 3 of their children, Lillie "Leah", Tomy and Daisy. Two step-children; Lottie May and Houston Jackson and, a nephew, George Wagner. Joe is 31 years old, he cannot read or write, speaks English. His profession is a sawmill laborer, he has been married for two years. He lives in a house that he is renting; the family residence is Corrigan Town, Polk County.

By April 1910 the US census lists Joe with his growing family, the number of children is six; in addition to Daisy, Lillie "Leah" and Tomy, it lists Willie, Harry and Wiley. Joe is now 41 years old.

Towns and sawmills Joe may have lived and worked for:

During 1890s, Corrigan Town, TX; Allen Lumber was one of 17 sawmills in the area.

1894-1902, Diboll, TX; Southern Pine Lumber Company

1903-04, Asia, TX; Allen & Williams Lumber

1905-1915, Carmona, TX; Carter Lumber, Kirby Lumber Companies

1916-1935, Lufkin, TX; Angelina County Lumber; other industries, Southland Paper Mills & Texas Foundries

Alice with son Harry and daughter Willie Ruth, 1957.

The US 1920 census dated in January of that year, finds Joe still in Polk County, living west of the HE&WT R/R, it may be in Carmona. The children listed are Harry, Wiley, Margaret and Carl; Alice and the children are listed as Mulatto. Joe is still renting, by this time he is able to read and write. Daughter Daisy is listed with her husband, Robert and baby, Lovi Dee living next door.

Joe moved his family from one sawmill town to the next, living in Polk and Angelina counties. He worked hard to save his money to buy them a home and he finally did by saving his money in an old syrup pail that he hung on a nail in the kitchen, he did not believe in saving his money in a bank. The most common job at the sawmill was that of laborer. In 1890 the rate of pay for common labor at the Angelina County Lumber Company was $1.25 to $1.50 a day for an eleven-hour day. Joe saved his money and eventually bought the home at 415 Fargo Street, Lufkin, Angelina County, Texas. Joe worked as a sawmill laborer for 45 years. Unfortunately there are no photographs of Grandpa Joe, his image is only in the memory of those who had the pleasure of knowing him.

The US 1930 census finds Joe working in Diboll, he is alone on this census, probably in Diboll to work, and the family is living in Lufkin by this time. This census list whether an individual is a veteran; Joe is listed, as not being a veteran, he had not been in any wars.

As determined from Joe's death certificate; he had lived in Lufkin for six years; the home in Lufkin was probably purchased in 1929. It lists his birthplace in San Jacinto County, Texas; his father's name is unknown, father's birthplace unknown, it lists his mother's name, Margurette Smith, her birthplace is unknown. Joe was attended by a physician from 1 April 1935 to 27 June 1935. Joe became ill on June 1st, he must have been ill for about 2 ½ months before his death. He died on the 27th of June and was buried the next day. Two of his sons signed the death certificate; Harry Smith and Wiley Smith.

William Odom

Joe died at the age of 66 on 27 June 1935, he is buried at Lufkin Land Cemetery, formerly known as Strangers Rest Cemetery; and before that it was called, Frost Cemetery, Lufkin, Texas.

Narratives/Memories from family about Grandpa:

Ruby Martin (granddaughter) tells this story of a conversation she overheard as a child between Grandpa Joe and Grandma Alice:

Grandpa said, "I'm gonna buy me a house". Grandma told him, "how you gonna buy a house making only a dollar fifty a day?" Grandpa told her, "if you don't think I can, then you'd better git yourself another nigger".

Ruth Martin (granddaughter) shares the following stories about Grandpa Joe: "My brother Solomon (Martin) loved to talk to his Grandpa; he would ask all kinds of questions and talk to Grandpa all night. When Grandpa would get enough, he would tell Solomon, "ok boy, I'm tired now, goodnight boy, I'm going to bed". "Grandpa had a beautiful voice and would sing before going to bed".

Ruth tells this story about Grandpa's dogs: "Grandpa Joe had this big, black German Sheppard, he liked dogs. He kept him in the yard. One morning Grandma Alice and Ruby (Martin), who was about 7 years old, went to pick blackberries. They returned to the house with their baskets full of berries. Grandma went in first and Ruby was following, before she could get inside the gate, that big, black dog jumped her and knocked the berries out of her hand and bit her hand and arm badly. She cried out and Grandpa came and got that dog and beat him, almost to death. From that day on, Ruby would have nothing to do with dogs, except to feed our mama's many dogs whenever she was out of town".

Alice's earliest origins can be found on the US 1880 census. She is, at the age of five, listed with her mother, Hulda Odom, her sister Laura Odom and brother William Odom, possibly the "white man", who rode up on a horse to visit grandma. The census lists the children as mulatto; their mother is listed as a Black, widowed farmer from the state of Virginia. Both Hulda's parents, Alice's grandparents were born in Virginia. The maiden name of Odom was confirmed by at least two family members; son Houston's death certificate, daughter Leah's death certificate and also on Joe and Alice's marriage record.

Joe married Alice in 1898, rather they had hoped to marry but according to the marriage record issued by the state of Texas, the marriage ceremony was never executed. There are all sorts of possibilities for this; maybe the minister didn't return the license as he should have, something happened to prevent them completing the ceremony, or the fee/bond may have been too expensive for them to pay. Whatever the reason, they attempted to legitimize their union and created a record for descendants to find. In their hearts and minds they were man and wife until death parted them. Alice Odom-Smith, passed away on the 24 September

1960, at the age of 86. She died at the home of her daughter Leah in Lufkin. She was a member of the Church of God; she was buried at Cedar Grove Cemetery, Lufkin. At that time Alice was survived by two daughters; Leah and Willie, three sons; Tomy, Harry and Wiley; 14 grandchildren and 20 great-grandchildren.

Various family members repeat stories of grandma's origins; her mother was a slave, Grandma's "brother", "father", who was a white man, would ride up on a horse to visit her in Lufkin. This white stranger never entered her home and she never told anyone his name or where he came from.

Joe P. Gregory (grandson) states, "Grandma told me that her mother was a slave."

Marine Smith (granddaughter) says, a white man would ride up on a horse and ask us children who were playing in the yard, "Is Lil Allie here?" She further states, "We would run and get grandma and she would sit out on the porch and visit with this white man, who looked to be about the same age as grandma, she never told us who he was, this was in the late 1930s, we were all little kids."

L.C. Smith (grandson) tells his stories about Grandma: "I was just a little boy, six or seven years old??"

"She was my protector, my Daddy (Harry Smith), would whip me and Grandma would try to stop him by standing between us. "Well, one time she got in the way and was too late for Daddy to stop and she got hit, she didn't stand in the way after that."

"Grandma would take me with her when she went downtown, Lufkin. We would go to the hardware store and Grandma was kin to the owner of the store because she would go in the back and sit down for a visit while we were in the store. I don't remember the name of the store or the man's name that she visited with."

The Lufkin (Texas) News, September 26, 1960 Page 2; Courtesy of Angelina County Genealogical Society, Lufkin,

Ruby Jo Mayfield (great-granddaughter): "I don't recall how old I was when I met her, but I was around four years old when I was aware of anything. Grandma lived in Lufkin, in her home with her son Harry and his family. She didn't drive a car and she didn't work outside the home. Grandma was a likeable person, very firm and spoke with a heavy voice for such a tiny lady. She enjoyed cooking and listening to Dr. Herbert W. Armstrong (Church of God), on the radio. She used to cook fish a lot for me, mostly catfish. She also loved to cook brains (beef). I loved her cooking; I would eat the fish up as fast as she cooked it."

"Grandma would visit us in Beaumont, staying with Mama (Willie) for three months at a time. When she would get tired of me running in and out of the house, she would put a stuffed animal in front of every door to the house to keep me away. I was really afraid of stuffed animals. That was my only dislike. Grandma Alice wore dresses all the time, I never saw her in pants. Her dresses were full in length. Her shoes were what we call "old folks comforts". The shoe lace went all the way to the top, which were high top shoes. I can't recall Grandma mentioning any family members long gone or any parents. In later years Grandma's health began to fail and she developed cataracts on her eyes, where she went blind. That grieved her so, when she lost her eyesight."

Cynthia Hawkins (great-granddaughter):

"I first met great-grandmother Alice during a family vacation to Texas the summer of 1957. My father drove from California to Texas and other states to visit our relatives. On this trip we had the pleasure of traveling to Lufkin to visit our great-grandmother for the first time that I can remember. She lived in a small house in a neighborhood with other houses similar to hers. As I recall the house was made from dark wood, it wasn't painted and she had an "out house" in the backyard and further out there was a well for drinking water and other things. We met Uncle Tomy, he lived with Grandma."

"In addition to Uncle Tomy living with her, Harry another son, and his family came to live with her. We met Uncle Harry and one of his daughters', Corrine, that summer. Corrine had a twin sister named Marine". "I remember that Grandma was a very tiny little lady, I was a child and she was barely as tall as me. She wore a cotton dress with an apron over it. She was making a quilt and when she hugged me a pin stuck me. She didn't have teeth in her mouth and she was "dipping snuff" and she had a corn cob pipe."

Gwendolyn Broussard, Jody (great-granddaughter) "I first met Grandma Alice in Beaumont during the summer I was about eight years old. She came to visit Mama Willie and the rest of the family. Grandma Alice spoke very softly and Mama Willie seemed so happy to have her visit. Grandma Alice lived in Lufkin. I don't remember much except the drive to her house was very long. My uncle Harry (#2), drove us there. My first visit to her home was in the winter, around the holidays. That's where I met Aunt Leah and Uncle Harry (#1). Having aunts meant the world to me, Aunt Leah had a very pretty smile, and she seemed to have a wonderful sense of humor. I don't remember too many other folks. Everybody seemed to really like the name Jo Helen."

Chapter 3

Lottie to Daniel

Joe and Alice together would have twelve children, the record of all the children's names and dates of birth were recorded in a family Bible belonging to their daughter Willie Ruth. In the Bible she writes, "My Darling Mother and all her children". Ironically, the Bible does not list her father. The Bible is located in Beaumont, Texas.

The Wiergate commissary was an important center of activity for sawmill workers and their families. *Courtesy of the Newton History Center, Newton, Texas.*

In every lumber town, separated from the main area by the log pond, the railroad tracks, or the mill itself, was the "quarter".

This was the part of the company town set aside for the Black workers in the mill, the yard, the construction gangs, and the logging crew. There they and their families lived, completely segregated as in other southern towns at the turn of the century (1900).

Housing for Black families, was the most inferior quality. The houses were similar to smaller houses in the white section except that they were seldom kept in repair. The usual style was the unpainted three or four-room box built of rough lumber with a board or shingle roof. Not only were the houses poorer than those in the white section, but the "quarter" was less well drained and had few or no trees and few plots for vegetable gardens. Almost no houses had running water, and several houses shared a single water faucet in the yard. Inside the typical house had only a single pine floor, unfinished walls and ceilings, broken windows and a leaky roof. For this the Black worker paid four to six dollars a month, and the rent was often collected weekly.

There were usually both a church and a school in the "quarter," built by the company but after that ignored. Recreation in the "quarter" was even more limited than in the main section of the town. Any sports or games that the Blacks played they played among themselves. To most of the residents of the company town, especially the wives and children the center of interest and activity was not the mill, but the commissary.

Lottie May Jackson

DOB: 3 August 1891, Ewing, TX—DOD: Unknown

Parents: Houston Jackson 1st, Alice Odom

Lottie May, oldest child of Alice and step-daughter to Joe Smith. Sometimes was identified as L.M. Jackson, as she was listed in the Family Bible. Lottie left home when she was very young. She was just 15 years old when she met and married Jake Howard, (Polk Co. Index), on 24 December 1906. Lottie was the daughter of Houston Jackson the 1st, as noted on the death certificate of Houston Jackson, 2nd. It is not known if Lottie and Jake ever had any children.

Lottie left home at a young age and there is no evidence that she ever returned. She shows up in Galveston along with her spouse listed as James M. Howard, in 1920. James or Jake, was employed with the Pullman Company as a porter. Lottie was 28 years old at that time, they lived in a boarding home along with many other employees of the Pullman Company.

No record has been located of Lottie's death, although she might be buried along with other family members at Lufkin Land Cemetery in Lufkin.

Houston Jackson, 2nd

DOB: 13 January 1893—DOD: 27 December 1928

Parents: Houston Jackson 1st, Alice Odom

They called him "Honey", Uncle Honey and Huse. His name was Houston Jackson, oldest son of Alice and Houston 1st, step-son of Joe Smith. He was born in Ewing, Texas, he was a sawmill laborer all his

Houston & Bessie Jackson

life. In 1919 he married Miss Bessie Boss and lived in various east Texas sawmill towns. At some point he was no longer married and would visit his sister Willie and sometimes lived with her and her family in Deweyville, Texas.

In 1928 Uncle Honey had returned to his birth place, Ewing, where he died of heart complications as a result of malaria fever. He was 35 years old. He never had any children. He is buried in Lufkin.

Ruth Martin (Niece) tells a memory of her uncle:

"I believe I was about seven years, Solomon was nine or ten, and Ruby was five or six. Uncle Honey lived with us in Deweyville, I don't remember for how long. He worked for the saw mill. He liked to read the newspaper; we would hit the paper and run. He had married a second time and his wife's name was Bessie. Honey left Deweyville before us, he went to Ewing, and he got real sick and went back to Ewing where Grandma Alice lived. Grandma and Grandpa Joe took care of him. They set up his bed outside in the summertime for it was more comfortable for him to sit up in his bed and sleep outside."

Lillie "Leah" Smith

DOB: 31 July 1895—DOD: 14 February 1974

Parents: Joe Smith, Alice Odom

Leah is what she was called by all who knew her, but her name was Lillie, according to the Family Bible and the US 1900 census, as she was listed with her parents. Leah was born in 1895 in Diboll, Texas. She worked as a laundress, people would drop off their clothes for her to wash and iron. She had no children of her own, although she was step-mother to her 2nd husband, Mr. Tolbert's three daughters and a favorite Auntie to many nieces and nephews. In a letter written 18 May 1971, to niece Ruth Martin, she thanks her for a "Mother's Day" card and also mentions receiving a call from niece Corrine, Harry (#1's) daughter.

Leah's first husband was named Buck Mott, an older gentleman, who according to niece Ruth Martin, "Mr. Mott was very mean to Aunt Leah, she married him when she was very young". Leah eventually left Mr. Mott and married Mr. Melvin Tolbert, a man from Louisiana.

Leah was a member of the Order of Eastern Star, Annie Jones Chapter No. 114. She attended the Church of the Living God on O'Quinn Street in Lufkin, Bishop Moss was her pastor. Aunt Leah passed away on Valentine's Day in 1974.

Memories of Aunt Leah:

L.C. Smith (nephew)

"Aunt Leah would go to Beaumont (to visit her sister Willie) and stay every year. Leah didn't drive, cause she liked to drink, Uncle Melvin would drive her. I loved to hear her talk; she loved to tell "tall tales". "Aunt Leah, my Daddy (Harry#1), and a neighbor would sit on the long porch in Lufkin and tell us tall tales and ghost stories. Aunt Leah's stories were like telling us "there's money buried in the ground and if you get close to it, it moved". Aunt Leah didn't work, Uncle Melvin took good care of her, sometimes she took in ironing, but Uncle Melvin worked at Texas Foundry a good job at the steel mill."

Tom Charles Smith

DOB: 28 October 1897—DOD: 13 March 1965

Parents: Joe Smith, Alice Odom

Tom Charles Smith, "Uncle Tomy" too many, liked to drink moonshine. He kept a jug of it hidden under Grandma Alice's porch in the back of the house. Young Harry Gregory discovered his uncle's hiding place when he was a child, playing at Grandma's house. Uncle Tomy had a wife named Ruth, he had been married twice, the 2nd wife's name is unknown.

Memories/Stories about Uncle Tomy:

Ruth Martin (niece)

"Uncle Tomy and wife, Ruth lived in Beaumont for a while and he worked and saved his money to buy Ruth a house. Well, Ruth took the money and went to Louisiana. Uncle Tomy followed, hoping to live with her in Louisiana, but Ruth's brothers ran him off. He returned to Texas, he stayed for a time in Beaumont with us and worked as a sawmill laborer. He had no children."

"Poor Uncle Tomy returned to Lufkin to care for his mother after Grandpa died in 1935. He said, "I'm gonna stay here til the wagon comes". A few years later, another son came to live with Grandma. Harry#1, his wife Mary Ella and children came to live in Lufkin. After Grandma Alice died, Uncle Tomy was limited to living in the kitchen area of the home. Harry and Mary Ella built another kitchen in the home for their use. The living areas of the home were off limits to Tomy, even though Harry had built a bathroom in the home, Tomy had to continue to use the "out house". When Willie, his sister would come to visit, she would make everyone sit outside on the porch to visit with Uncle Tomy. Uncle Tomy experience poor health, he caught pneumonia and at some point suffered a fall, he died as a result of injuries to his head."

L.C. Smith speaks about his uncle,

"Uncle Tomy lived in Seattle (Washington) for a time and he told me he had been in the Army. He also told me that he had a son living in Seattle. I was just a little boy when he told me that." "Uncle Tomy lived at Grandma's house with us when I was a boy. He slept in the kitchen. We had two kitchens. Grandma had a kitchen and my Daddy built a kitchen for my mother."

Tomy was discovered by nephew, young L.C. Smith, in the woods not far from Grandma's house. He had fallen and hit his head and was unconscious lying on the ground in the rain. He was brought back to the house, he developed pneumonia and later died as a result of his injuries.

Daisy Smith

DOB: 6 March 1900—DOD: Unknown

Parents: Joe Smith, Alice Odom

Daisy Smith, just 4 years older than her sister Willie, first appeared on the US 1900 census listed with her parents, living in Corrigan Town, Polk County, Texas. She was only two months old at the time. By the US 1910 census, she is ten years old and still living in Polk County.

Daisy is married at the age of 16 to Robert Martin (no relation to Lee), a sawmill laborer, as listed on the Polk County 1916 Marriage Index. Four years later Daisy is listed with her spouse and one child, named Lovi Dee. She continues to live in Polk County, west of the HE&WT R/R, on Carrington and Groveton Road. She is also next door to her parents, and the brothers and sisters, still living at home, in January 1920. Daisy's baby is 22 months old and that is the last time Daisy shows up on a census. She disappears, and sister Willie always told the story of Daisy being poisoned by her mother-in-law and dying at a very young age.

Daisy's only child, Lovi Dee grew up in Texas with relatives and as an adult moved to Seattle, Washington. Lovi Dee never had any children of her own.

Daniel Smith

DOB: 18 May 1902—DOD: Unknown

Parents: Joe Smith, Alice Odom

Daniel is listed in the Family Bible by his sister, Willie, stating that he was born in 1902. He was born two years too late to show up on the U S 1900 census and by the US 1910 census, he does not show up, the reason is unknown. Although it is quite possible that Daniel died as a child. Childhood mortality rates were not good for that period in our history, especially for Black children. It may be that Daniel died due to small pox, tuberculosis or some other disease.

Daniel was the 6th child for Alice, he was the older brother born two years before his sister Willie. Daniel may be buried at the same cemetery as his father, Lufkin Land Cemetery, Lufkin, Texas.

Chapter 4

Willie to Carl

Willie Ruth Smith

DOB: 28 September 1904 – DOD: 20 February 1997

Parents: Joe Smith, Alice Odom

Model-T similar to the one Willie drove to deliver lunches. Photo taken near Weirgate. Courtesy of the Newton History Center, Newton, TX.

In September 1904, Theodore "Teddy" Roosevelt was the President of the United States. The popular books for that period included two by prominently known scholars, activist and black authors; "The Souls of Black Folks", by W.E.B Dubois and "Up From Slavery", by Booker T. Washington. A loaf of bread cost four cents, milk was 29 cents a gallon, a brand new car cost five hundred dollars, the Ford Model-T had just recently been invented and in Asia, Texas a daughter was born to Joe and Alice, they named her Willie Ruth.

Willie Ruth Smith

Willie like her brothers and sisters grew up in various sawmill towns, attending schools provided by the mill, her Papa (as they called him), probably worked for the Allen & Williams Lumber Company, in Asia. Later the family lived for a time in Carmona, Texas there were two mill towns she could have lived in; Carter Lumber had a town or the town provided by the Kirby Lumber Company.

Willie left home at the early age of 15; marriage was her escape, from the harsh upbringing that she experienced with her father. A man, who believed in whipping his children until they bled, Willie wanted to continue her education, according to other family members, "she always wanted to be a school teacher". That was not to be, although, she taught her father to read, by reading from the Bible.

October 2, 1919, at the age of fifteen, Willie married Lee Martin. They were married in Trinity County as confirmed in the Trinity County Marriage Index 1919, Lee's birthplace. They started their young married lives in Voth, Jefferson County Texas, probably because that's where Lee found work. Lee was, like so many mill laborers, driven by his employment, as Willie would endure during their marriage.

In April 1920 Lee, Willie and Lee's brother Howard Martin, lived in a boarding house in Beaumont (US 1920 census). February 24, 1921, Lee and Willie's first child was born. A son, they named Solomon Lee Martin. Still on the move, by the time their second child was born, Ruth Mae on March 7, 1923, they were in Ragley, Texas. Not long after on August 15, 1924, another daughter was born, Ruby Lee, in Hochel, Texas. During this time Willie worked hard raising her children and packing and unpacking, whenever Lee's temper would drive him to quit a job and move to the next town. Lee would hop the freight trains for a ride to the next town, find work and send for Willie and the children. She kept busy working at whatever jobs she could find to help support the family. In Deweyville, she had a car that she drove, a Model "T". Willie would deliver the lunches, prepared by the men's wives, to the Black laborers working at the lumber mill. Ruth says, "my daddy, Lee worked on what was called the slaughter pen, it was like a ferry, it moved going up and down and as it moved down it drops the wood in the water. We children, saw this we would walk to school right past the mill and see the men load the lumber on the pen. We would stop sometimes and watch it." Ruth's comments about Deweyville (Texas), "we had a commissary, one big commissary, we bought things with script instead of money. They sold everything there; clothes, food, tools, material for sewing. The town had a church, a little wooden church built in the "quarters". I went to grade school in Deweyville, your Aunt Ruby was allowed to sit in class with me when she was five years old.

In the early 1930s Lee left Willie and the children again, this time in Trinity, when Lee came back for them, they had moved. Shortly thereafter Willie had married her next door neighbor, Mr. Perry Lewis Gregory, a much older man. Joe Perry Gregory was born 28 March 1934 and her last child, another son, Harry Lewis Gregory was born on, 8 August 1936. Willie's 2nd husband Perry Gregory, they called him "Mr. Po Boy", was born in 1871, in Texas, his father's name was Silas

Lee Martin

Gregory, information about his mother is unknown. Perry Lewis Gregory was listed on the US 1920 census, living at Lovelady Road, in Trinity, along with his first wife, Ida. From that marriage he had two daughters; Lenora and Gertrude. He was employed as a sawmill laborer. Eventually, he was single again and married Willie (Smith) Martin.

Mr. Po Boy was a Baptist deacon, step-daughter Ruth says, "At night we attended the Baptist Church, up the hill from where we lived". "Po Boy" was known for his beautiful singing voice, he loved to sing, "His Eye Is on the Sparrow". Mr. Po Boy was well respected in his church community because he was very skillful at fundraising. He was known for getting donations from the white folks and taking credit for the donations. He was not kind to Willie's older children. Ruth tells this story, "this day it was real hot outside and Solomon had to tote a heavy wagon of wood back and forth from a long distance to and from the house, over and over". Ruth says, "every time he (Solomon), got to the house he would fall out and say, "Mama please can I stop now? Solomon couldn't stop until Po Boy told him he could. Ruth states his cruelty towards her, "he liked to scare me with his pistol. One time he scared me so bad that I ran away from the house, hiding so close that I could hear my mama and Wee Wee calling me and looking for me, but I was too afraid to come out." "One time" Ruth continues, "Mama sent me to the commissary in town, and while there I saw Mr. Po Boy giving some money to this woman. He saw me and even though when I got home, I didn't have a chance to tell Mama what I had seen, but when Po Boy came in he just started beating me, he tried to beat me to death. Mama wasn't satisfied after that."

Willie sent Solomon first, to New Williard to Lee and Lee's mother Carrie, Ruth and Ruby soon followed. Willie would join them months later with Joe and Harry. They lived with Lee and his mother, Grandma Carrie and they would visit Lee's relatives in the country, in Kittrel, Texas. They called him Big Jack Armstead, he was Grandma Carrie's brother. He had a ranch and a lot of land. There were other Armstead relatives; Aunt Delphi was Grandma Carrie's sister. Ruth says, "On one visit while we were in Kittrel, Mama went to Trinity to get some of her things that she had left and she wanted to go to the house while Mr. Po Boy was at work. Lee's brothers took her and she picked up her things and left before Po Boy returned. That was the last time I remember visiting our relatives in Kittrel."

Willie was located on the US 1940 census, living in Beaumont on Fletcher Street. Solomon was 19 years old, Ruth 15 years, Ruby 14, Joe was 6 years and Harry was 3 years old. She was listed a Negro, widowed, head of household, she was thirty-five years old. Willie continued to work hard to support her children, Solomon helped out by working after school and eventually quitting school to work full-time to support the family. Ruth also worked at different jobs to help out. Ruby completed high school, she helped her mother at home cooking and helping with her younger brothers. In Beaumont Willie went to work for American National Bank, she worked in maintenance at nights.

Willie would marry again, to Mr. Mike Gant. He wanted Willie to put her two younger sons, by then the only ones left at home, Joe and Harry, out. He said, "feed them bread and coffee water". She divorced him, he found out when someone told him about the newspaper notice. Mike could not read that well. He met Willie when she was leaving work and asked, "what's dis here Willie? Holding up the newspaper", Mike was a refinery worker.

Willie was very protective of her children and wanted them around her all her life. She had experienced the deaths of all her brothers and sisters, some to tuberculosis, malaria fever and poisoning. The poisoning of her sister, Daisy, made her very reluctant to eat anyone's cooking, it was very late in life when she would eat from fast food restaurants like KFC or Churches' Chicken. Willie was very dedicated to her church and her favorite department was Sunday School, her religious influence was inherited by all of her children and many grandchildren, who are very active in their churches. She was a lifelong member of the Church of the Living God, CWFF, in Lufkin and Beaumont. Willie passed away on 20 February 1997, at the age of 92. She is buried at Sacred Heart Cemetery, Beaumont, Texas. Willie's desires were met, in that all of her children were with her in life and at the time of her death. She was blessed to see all of them grow to old age and have children of their own. She departed this life with all of her children by her side.

Memories/Narrative from family:

Ruth Martin (daughter) tells this story about her mother, "In Beaumont during the 1940s, Black folks riding the bus had to sit behind a sign that said, "Colored". On this particular day Mama came home and told us, "all the Black seats were taken and I just went and sat next to this white lady and we struck up a conversation and we talked all the way to my stop, no one said anything to us".

Gwendolyn Broussard "JoHelen" (granddaughter) remembers,"Mama Willie worked at a bank in the evenings. She would walk to work sometimes with Ms. Tibbodeux. Aunt Ruby and Uncle Harry (#2) would take turns picking her up. I like going for the ride so I could see the very shiny building and the large clock. My friends would laugh at Mama Willie's yard shoes, but not before she gave them candy. Everybody in the projects loved my Grandma. Her favorite color was blue. I know we ate a lot of fried chicken, so that's got to be her favorite. Mama liked watching the Lawrence Welk Show and some of the Black stars on Ed Sullivan; Ray Charles, Harry Belafonte, Lena Horne and Mahalia Jackson. Mama's favorite music was hymns and spirituals. She prayed all the time, even when we came over to beg for candy, all my friends had to pray too."

"I always felt safe around Mama Willie. She knew what to do to cheer me up. I have so many memories. Mama (Willie) wasn't good at keeping a secret. My Dad, (Joe Gregory), had bought me a shiny new bike for Christmas Mama (Willie) said, if I didn't tell, I could ride it right now in the backyard. So every day before Christmas, I would go over and ride the bike. Then on Christmas Eve when I went to get the bike, we both let out a great big laugh, and act surprised, we had to share the laugh with Aunt Ruby!"

Harry Smith

DOB: 28 December 1905 – DOD: 18 March 1969

Parents: Joe Smith, Alice Odom

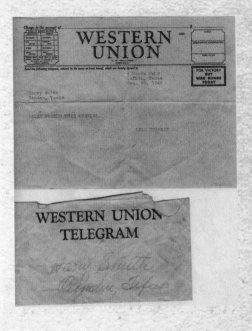

Harry was born in Carmona, Texas. Harry worked the early part of his life in Camden as stated on the US 1930 census, he was still single and living as a boarder in the home of Maude Williams. He was twenty-four at that time. Harry applied for his social security card at the age of thirty, in Camden. He worked for W.T. Carter & Brother Lumber Company. He married Mary Ella Saddler and together they had five children, including a set of twin girls Marine and Corrine. Harry also, fathered a daughter, named Dorothy, prior to starting his family with Mary Ella. Harry was still living in Camden in 1946, when he received word via telegram, from sister, Leah that their cousin Helen (Knighton), had passed.

Harry and his family eventually moved in with Grandma Alice to help take care of her. Grandma's house had a well and an outhouse. Harry dug the well; he built a kitchen on the back. Originally it was a three room house, skillful carpenter that he was; Harry built additional rooms to accommodate his large family. He also, built another kitchen for his wife. "Grandma had her kitchen and Mama, (Mary Ella) had her kitchen" as son L.C. Smith tells it, "Daddy built a kitchen on the back, Grandma had a kitchen, but Mama and Grandma couldn't get along with the same kitchen. Mama had a kitchen and Grandma had a kitchen". "Daddy worked for Angelina Lumber mill and Grand Oak, they made doors", says L.C. Smith.

L.C. Smith (son) tells of family life in Lufkin,

"Mama cooked fish, chicken, okra gumbo, lima beans, collard greens and sweet potatoes. I thought I'd never eat another collard green when I grew up. We had a garden out back, we raised our own hogs, raised our own meat. We had chickens, no cows in Lufkin, we had cows in Camden. Oh, we had one cow, I remember . . . . I left a calf with Wiley(#2), when I left home. You have to get that story from Wiley(#2) (laughs).""We got together on Christmas and Daddy's birthday, it was in December and my other grandpa's birthday. We always had a big dinner. Most of the relatives didn't have to come far, they were already there. Mama's sisters and Aunt Willie seemed like Uncle Melvin would go get her."

"Daddy was a hunter, he loved to go hunt, every now and then he'd fish, but he'd hunt coons, squirrels, deers, we ate possum, coons and rabbits, no armadillo though." Harry Smith at age 24 is living as a boarder in Camden, Texas as listed on the U.S. 1930 Census. Harry and Mary Ella's growing family is still living in Polk County, by 1940, in Camden. They have four children. The twin girls; Marine and Corrine are 5 years old, A.J. the oldest son is four years old and youngest son L.C. is three. The 1940 census reveals that Harry completed 4th grade, is living in a rented home. He works as a sawmill laborer earning $624.00 per year, in 1939 he worked 40 hours a week for 52 weeks.

L. to R. Mary Ella and Harry Smith

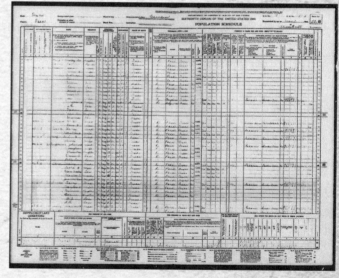

Source Information: Ancestry.com. 1940 United States Federal Census (database on-line), Provo, UT, USA: Ancestry.com Operations, Inc. 2012, Original data: United States of America, Bureau of the Census, Sixteenth Census of the United States, 1940. Washington, D.C.; National Archives and Records Administration, 1940, 4,643 rolls.

Florida Faye Bailey

Wiley Smith (#1)

DOB: 10 August 1908 – DOD: 21 December 1974

Parents: Joe Smith, Alice Odom

They called him "Sugar", he liked the women and they liked him too. According to niece, Marine Smith, "Uncle Wiley was a ladies man; he was dapper, meaning he dressed real nice, all the women ran after him. He was called "Sugar" cause he just was so sweet, sugar dripped off him."

Wiley, was a young man during World War I and he worked for the Conservation Corps. The Corps provided much needed jobs for young men to work on government projects; repairing roads, bridges, forestry, etc. Wiley lived for a time in Sabine, Texas working at a saw mill. He returned to Lufkin, where he worked for Angelina County Lumber Company, as a saw mill laborer, later the company was bought by Owens Illinois, the company that Wiley eventually retired from. He married Florida Faye "Aunt Floyd" Bailey and helped to raise her son, Joe Clyde. Wiley's only child, a daughter named Rose, was born before his marriage to Florida, her mother's name was Jurlene.

Wiley was a Mason, a member of Dawn of Light Masonic Lodge, he and Florida attended Goodwill Baptist Church, where he served on the Senior Usher Board, Reverend A.D. Thomas was his pastor.

Wiley passed away on Saturday, 21 December 1974, after a lengthy illness at a local hospital. He was 66 years old. Florida Faye Bailey, Wiley's wife of many years, passed away on Friday 23 September 2005.

Wiley "Sugar" Smith

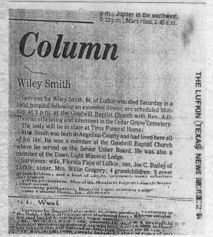

Memories/Narratives from family: Ruth Martin (niece) remembers, "Uncle Wiley played baseball, he was on a Negro team in Lufkin. I remember, I was a teenager and he would come to Grandma's house to change into his grey and white pinstriped uniform. I don't know why his uniform was at Grandma's but for whatever reasons, he would change at Grandma's and go to the park to play baseball. I never saw him play."L.C. Smith (nephew) recalls his uncle, "Sugar! (Laughs), well he was just a hard worker. He's got a kid too, a girl, can't remember her name Sugar's step-son is Joe Bailey; he's been around Lufkin a long time".

Margarett Smith

DOB: 01 July 1911 – DOD: Unknown

Parents: Joe Smith, Alice Odom

Margarett or Margurite, was the youngest daughter of Alice and Joe. They called her "granny", though her looks were far from old. Oral family history dictates that she was said to have been very beautiful, with long dark hair. She was the "belle of the ball". She had many suitors (boyfriends). She was very sociable and liked to go to parties. She didn't keep the same man for too long. She finally settled down with Mr. Ulysees Knighton long enough to produce a daughter, Helen Harriet Knighton. Unfortunately, Margarett died young, the exact date is not known, she was the first child of Alice and Joe to die from tuberculosis, she passed away as best as can be determined prior to the 1940s.

Marine Smith when asked did she know Margarett? "Yes, Helen's mother, we would visit (Lufkin) but stay with Grandma for a while, when she (Margarett) got sick, we couldn't go back up there. We were about 5-7 years old, along like that, when she would send us home, cause we love to go see Grandma and we really didn't get to know Helen and Margarett. We didn't get much chance to be around them because Grandma would have to wash everything down, so we wouldn't get TB. I remember when she was real little, Helen, all I remember about Margarett when she was sick in bed, she had a head full of hair."

(This information is based on interviews with nieces; Ruth and Ruby Martin, 2004-2006 and Marine Smith 2010.)

Carl Smith

DOB: 20 March 1914 – DOD: unknown, after 1940

Parents: Joe Smith, Alice Odom

Carl Smith was born in 1914, too late for the 1910 census, but by the US 1920 census, he is listed along with siblings; Harry, Wiley and Margarett and his parents. As noted in the Family Bible, Carl is the last child for Joe and Alice, to survive. The last sibling was born and died the same day in 1916, as noted in the Bible belonging to Willie Ruth.

Carl is listed in 1920 at the age of five. He was living with the rest of the family in Polk County. The family disappears and Joe is the only one located on the US 1930 census, in Diboll. Joe may have been working in Diboll and the family may have been at another location.

Carl is located twenty years later on the US 1940 census; he is by this time twenty-six years old. This census reveals that Carl had been married, divorced and had returned home to his mother. Carl's niece, Helen (Margarett's daughter), is now living with Grandma Alice, also. Carl is working as a hotel porter with a yearly salary of $250.00. There is no further evidence that has surfaced to determine what happened to Carl.

Chapter 5

Texas 1920s to 1940s

Daisy, Margarett and Wiley's Children

Negroes in Texas continued to gain a foot hold on a normal life for themselves and their children; they consistently fought for their rights in Texas through the Republican and third parties and by appeals for federal action in Congress or the courts. Yet they could not stop the racist policies created so strongly throughout the South at the turn of the century. Because of a smaller percentage of Black population, Texas did not have to follow many other southern states in the adoption of literacy tests and grandfather clauses. There were other ways to keep Black voter participation at a minimum; the decline in Black voter participation from about 100,000 in the 1890s to approximately 5,000 in 1906 suggest the effectiveness of the white primary, the poll tax became required in 1902, also, the "lily white" increase in the Republican party and the Klu Klux Klan.

On the job front, unskilled and semi-skilled jobs increased while agricultural and domestic workers declined. Personal and domestic services such as servants, laundresses, nurses and mid-wives, restaurant and saloon keepers, hair dressers, and barbers did compose 28 percent of all employed Negroes in 1900. Younger domestic servants, born after slavery, showed greater independence in seeking better jobs or wages.

For Joe and Alice's grandchildren most of which were born during this time of change and innovation for the United States. Entered the 1st World War in 1914, their fathers or uncles may have fought, creating African American veterans who fought a war in Europe, while still fighting for freedom and equal rights in their own country. This generation would be the children of the Prohibition Era in 1918, which created bootleg liquor and what folks called, "moonshine". Warren G. Harding would become the President during their lifetime, Calvin Coolidge the next. Many inventions and advances in medicine: Sound movies in 1926, television in 1928, insulin for diabetics, penicillin is discovered in 1928. These grandchildren would grow up to be young adults during the Great Depression, experience the 2nd World War and some would go off and fight in that war and Franklin D. Roosevelt was their President.

For the youngest of Joe and Alice's grandchildren the ones born in the 1930s and 1940s, life was ever changing and advances being made for their generations. One of the most dramatic developments that took place during the 1930s was the realignment of black voters. Blacks in large numbers switched their votes to the Democratic Party, deserting the party of Lincoln that Blacks supported since Reconstruction. This shift took place partly as a result of Blacks' involvement in labor unions that generally supported the Democrats and partly in response to Republican efforts to attract Southern segregationists. By the 1934 congressional elections, two years after Roosevelt won the presidency, most Blacks voted Democratic for the first time. This generation would remember the name of Jesse Owens, Gold Medal winner at the Berlin Olympics; the Negro Baseball Leagues was one of their forms of entertainment. Joe Louis becomes the heavyweight boxing champion of the world, Jackie Robinson becomes the first African American to break the color barrier and be allowed to play in the major leagues. They would be the generations to live in homes with running water, toilets instead of outhouses, ice boxes, not yet refrigerators or freezers. There would probably be a radio in every home and maybe a telephone, and this is probably the "first" generation to participate in the Great Migration, leaving the south or in this case, Texas, for jobs and lives in the East, West or Northern cities of the U.S. Here are their stories.

Daisy's Child – Lovi Dee Martin

DOB: 16 December 1916 – DOD: 6 September 1982

Lovi Dee, the only child of Robert and Daisy (Smith) Martin, born in Diboll. Lovi Dee lost her mother at a young age and was raised by family and adopted parents.

Cynthia's Narrative,

"I always wondered who Lovi Dee was, sure she was my mother's cousin. I knew that because my mother (Ruth Martin), told us about her. I liked her name, Lovi Dee, her parents named her for "love", I thought. My mother enjoyed traveling and loved visiting family wherever they lived. Lovi

Dee lived in Seattle, Washington. My mother would visit in the summer when school was out; I remember one of her trips in 1969-70. She took with her my then 4 year-old daughter and my little brother. Actually, Lovi Dee really came to life for me when I discovered her on the US 1920 census, there she was, living with her mother, Daisy and her father Robert Martin (no relation to Lee). Lovi Dee was only 22 ½ months old. The census also showed them living next door to Daisy's mother and father, and siblings still at home and yep, her parents were Joe and Alice Smith. It was for me like pieces of a puzzle that was beginning to fit." Lovi Dee's grandparents were my mom's grandparents too.

"My mother was not the only relative to keep in touch with Lovi Dee. At one time Uncle Tomy visited his niece in Seattle, a young Joe Gregory also spent summers with Lovi Dee, when she lived in Diboll, Texas. The story told was that Lovi Dee, having no children of her own, during a summer visit from young cousin Joe Gregory, Lovi Dee wanted to keep Joe and enroll him in school, but Willie was not to allow that. She sent Ruth, by bus, to bring him home. As a soldier in the US Army, Joe was stationed in Seattle, at some point and he spent weekends with his cousin."

"Another cousin, A.J. Smith, Harry (#1's) son, soon found his way to Seattle after graduating from high school. A.J. lived with Lovi Dee until he built a life there, for himself, in Seattle. Although Lovi Dee lost her mother (Daisy) at a very young age, strong family ties kept the cousins and other relatives close no matter where they lived." Lovi Dee Martin-Blake-Mosley, passed away on September 6, 1982 in Seattle, Washington.

Margarett's Child – Helen Harriet Knighton

DOB: 21 March 1927 – DOD: 20 January 1946

Parents: Ulysees Knighton, Margarett Smith

Helen was the only child born to Margarett and Ulysees Knighton. She kept a diary of her life during the early 1940s, writing with the innocence and optimism of a young teenage girl. No mention is made of her mother or father. Her mother may have already passed, and her father does not seem to be around.

She was a very social person writing of attending typical events for her age; basketball games, dances, going to the movies. She writes of being ill at times, but it is always referred to as a cold, not mentioning the tuberculosis that was beginning to ravage her body. Maybe she didn't know.

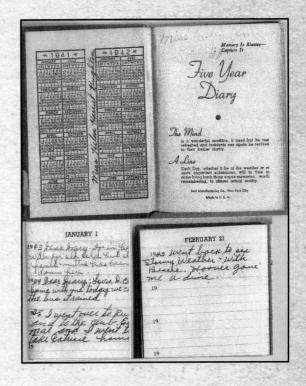

Helen does not seem to care about school very much, writing at some points of missing school but not disappointed. Although she did not write about school, she did complete her requirements to achieve her high school diploma, from Dunbar High School, actually receiving it before she died. Cousin, Ruth Martin states "the school gave the diploma to her early, believing that she would not live to receive it at the end of the school year". Helen shows up on the US 1940 census living with Grandma Alice and her Uncle Carl Smith. Helen passed away on 20 January 1946; she is buried at Lufkin Land Cemetery.

Excerpts from Helen's Diary . . . . transcribed by Cynthia (Helen's Diary was located at the home of Ruth Martin.)

Mar. 21, 1942—Dear Diary today is my birthday I've been in Joe quarters dancing Frankie and I had a swell time. My birthday dinner was swell

Jan. 1, 1943—Dear Diary I'm in bed with an old cold but it's my fault mittie has been down here.

Jan. 1, 1944—Dear Diary Lovie D. came home with me today we caught the bus it rained

Dec. 8, 1944—I've been to school got a letter from "Wee Wee" (Ruby Martin) she is going to marry I'm supposed to go

Dec. 15, 1944—Ruby & Raymond married tonight it was beautiful real lovely

Dec. 19, 1944—I washed and helped Aunt Willie cook

Dec. 20, 1944—I washed Uncle Sugar clothes and went over to" Wee Wee" house in the South End I had a nice time

Dec. 23, 1944—got my hair waved & curled went to town with Ruth heard the Grand Prize bell came here

Dec. 24, 1944—went to Sallies & Dew Drop Inn Breakfast dance starting at 12 until midnight

Jan. 19, 1945—went to the first basketball game, Earnest Slick & Oteas (sic) brought us home & their car (?) gave out

Feb. 20, 1945—went to see "Stormy Weather" It was really a good show K.D. sent me a pillow top & 3 handkerchiefs

Feb. 22, 1945—I haven't been anywhere. I'm sick with a cold. Aunt Leah & Mr. Melvin have been out here

Wiley (#1) Children:

Rose Smith—DOB: abt 1930 (unknown)

Parents: Wiley Smith & Jurlene Smith (no relation)

Currently, there is no information about Rose Smith, except that she is alive and lives in Texas.

Rose Smith

Joe Clyde Bailey

Parents: Wiley Smith, Florida Faye Bailey

Joe Clyde is the step-son raised by Wiley Smith and his mother Florida Faye. "JC" as the family calls him, is a life-long resident of Lufkin, Texas. He and his wife Lillie live in the same neighborhood that he grew up in. I was welcomed into their home on a recent visit to Lufkin (2010). JC has three children: Ira Louise, Donnie Richard and Rita Faye.

Joe Clyde and Lillie Bailey, Lufkin, Texas

Chapter 6

Solomon, Ruth, Ruby, Joe and Harry - Willie's Children

Willie with her children; L. to R. Ruby Lee, Harry Lewis, Joe Perry, Solomon Lee and Ruth Mae.

About Willie Ruth Smith –

My grandmother was a very strong, out-spoken, hardworking woman. She fiercely believed in God and quoted scriptures to all who knew her. She loved speaking in church and her favorite department was Sunday School. She was deeply religious, but she was no saint, she could on occasion curse with the best of them, had been known to grab her gun if she felt a situation warranted it. She loved animals especially dogs and had many in her lifetime. In her younger, early years, when I was a young child (1950s), she had chickens and ducks, she lived on Finis Street. I vividly remember the time she wrung a chicken's neck and that was supper for that day. I also remember everyone waiting up for her to return home from work, she worked nights at the bank and she was the center; everything revolved around her. I recall during "Hurricane Audrey", in 1957, how we all sat up late into the night; the kids had fun, playing with the melting candles, the adults were worrying about the storm, in the meantime, Gram said her prayers and good night, next we heard her snoring from her room. The next day we looked out into the yard and saw the large fig tree that sat in the middle of her yard, now pulled up by its roots. Shortly after the storm we celebrated July 4th at Galveston Beach. The part of the beach for the whites was destroyed by the storm; the amusement part with the concession stands all of the entertainment that was normally off limits to Blacks anyway. For us the side for the Blacks had nothing to destroy because there were no amusement rides or concession stands. We didn't miss the rides or concession stands, we entertained ourselves, we enjoyed the beach and our parents made a wonderful picnic lunch for us. I remember drinking a lot of Dr. Pepper sodas. The following are stories about her children and how she influenced their lives.

Solomon Lee Martin – DOB: 24 February 1921 – DOD: 22 August 2004

Solomon Lee Martin the oldest son of Lee and Willie was born on 24 February 1921, in New Willard, Texas. His early life was spent growing up in Volts, New Willard, Trinity and other mill towns. He was a teller of "tall tales", as many family members would describe him. Uncle Solomon's version of the same story always had more to it than anyone else's. His mouth got him into trouble, as a kid, his sisters Ruth and Ruby would come to his rescue on many occasions. Ruth tells the story of how Solomon would be in a hurry to walk to school in the mornings and his mother would tell him to wait for his sisters. He would leave anyway and Ruth and Ruby would find his books and belongings leaving a trail to school. He had gotten into trouble and had to run, leaving his belongings, they would pick them up. Ruth says, "When we got to school, Solomon would ask, did you get my books?" He was a very sociable guy, but he was no fighter. In later years, he would keep all who would listen, entertained with his "tall tales". Solomon almost died as a young child with malaria fever. According to sister, Ruth, "an old lady came to the house, we were at Grandma's (Alice) at the time, the lady mixed up a portion and gave it to Solomon and he got well". Solomon suffered most of his life with ear problems and deafness, wearing a hearing aid later in life. His hearing ailments kept him out of the military during World War II.

His favorite song was, "Let the Good Times Roll", he liked the ladies and had no shortage of girl friends. Solomon was a fashionable dresser; he wore suits, ties and hats, when he was not working. Sister Ruby enjoyed telling this story, "Solomon liked to dress up Joe and Harry, they were just little fellas, Solomon would clean them up from head to toe, all the while telling them that they "looked good" so when he finished getting them dressed, he would ask, "how do you look?" they would answer, "I look good!". Solomon's first job as a young man was with Owl Drug Store as a delivery boy, in Beaumont. He almost completed 12th grade, but interrupted school to continue to work to help support the family. The last job he had in Texas before leaving for California was with the U.S. Post Office in Beaumont. He met his first wife there, Lawrence Arthur. They married and moved to California, first living and working in Richmond, at the shipyards during World War II. Later he moved to San Francisco and began working for Southern Pacific Railroad, as a porter and a cook. He and Lawrence had one daughter, Cheryl Ann born in San Francisco, 31 January 1957. He was so happy to have a

Solomon Martin with 1st wife, Lawrence Arthur, S.F.

child at last; Cheryl was born to Solomon and Lawrence late in life because they never expected to have children. Cheryl was the light of his life; she grew into a fine young woman. She was a typical San Franciscan; she liked the big city, bright lights, life. Unfortunately, that life was to be cut short, Cheryl died in a tragic car accident.

Some years later, after the divorce from Lawrence, Solomon met and married Dorothy King, whom he was to learn, was his true "soul mate". They worked at Laguna Honda Hospital together. Dorothy quickly adapted to life with Solomon's family, gathering for family dinners, holidays and other social events, everyone loved Dorothy. From this marriage his second daughter, Tiffany was born on 12 July 1972 and he also accepted as his own, Dorothy's oldest daughter, Loretta. Solomon and Dorothy shared a happy life together until Dorothy's sudden death of a brain aneurysm on 16 December 1979. After Dorothy's death and upon retiring from Laguna Honda Hospital, he returned to Beaumont to live near his mother and his brothers and sister. Solomon enjoyed volunteering at the Senior Center and returning to his church roots, by attending the Church of the Living God, with his mother and spending time with the family. He enjoyed being with all his nieces and nephews. In his lifetime, Solomon married four times and fathered two daughters, he passed away on 22 August 2004, and he is buried at Sacred Heart Cemetery, Beaumont, Texas.

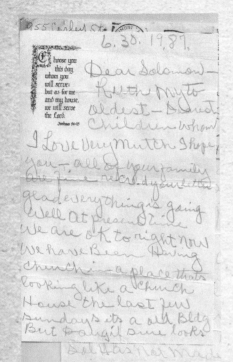

Willie loved and missed her two oldest children after they both moved to California. Ruth and Solomon and their families would travel to Texas for yearly vacations to visit their mother. Traveling in the summer by car, the men would take turns driving the highways to reach Texas in record time. Willie wrote to her children often, the following is an excerpt from one of her letters.

30 June 1987, postmarked 1 July 1987

Dear Solomon – Ruth my to (sic) oldest – dearest children whom I love very much. I hope you T (sic) all of your family are fine recvd your letter glad everything is going Well at present time. We are ok to right now We have been Having church in a place that's Looking like a church House

(She ends her letter with): Love to all, Mother WRG, Ans Soon, Ruthie – Sol

Cynthia Hawkins (Niece) recalls,

"I remember in the early 1950s Uncle Sol, they called him "Kid", would visit our family in Berkeley, California. He worked all week in San Francisco, for the rail road and on the weekends he jumped "sharp". He always dressed; the term then was "like a fashion plate". He wore the best suits with his gold watch on a chain. He always had a silver dollar for me and my sister. He liked to hunt; sometimes he would go hunting and bring our mother these awful looking rabbits that he caught. Ugh, I didn't like rabbit, my mother cooked them a few times, but I don't think they were a big hit with our family. I will always remember that he was one of the few adults that would, in later years when I was a teenage, let me practice how to drive in his car. By this time it was the 1960s and he had this little Ford Falcon "red". We lived in Richmond by then and I always looked forward to his visits, because he would give me the keys and I would go. I will always love him for that."

Sidney Brown, Cheryl Martin

"In the 1970s Uncle Solomon like so many at the time, got into the CB radio fad, talking from cars and trucks. He had a handle (CB name) and would talk on his CB radio with others. He really enjoyed that. He was also in his cowboy phase, he would dress up in his cowboy boots and hats, and he was wonderful." I was blessed to visit with my then 82-year old uncle one last time in the summer of 2004; he told me that he wanted to come visit us in California. We had a nice visit reminiscing about old times. He got sick a few weeks after we left and my Mom was still there visiting. They put him in the hospital and a nursing home for better care. My Mom and Aunt Ruby were with him when he told them, "get my clothes; I'm ready to go home". With his sisters by his bedside, he "went home", peacefully in his sleep on 22 August 2004.

Dionte Ramon Brown, Abt. 13 mos. old

Solomon Martin's Children and Grandchildren: Cheryl Ann Martin, was the only child of Solomon and Lawrence Martin. She attended primary and secondary schools in the San Francisco school district. Cheryl was a very likeable young lady and loved to party. She grew up in San Francisco and loved big city life. Cheryl left home at an early age and married an older man, Sidney Brown. From this marriage two children were born, Dionte, a son and Shante, a daughter. Cheryl's young life was cut short by a fatal car accident at the age of twenty-one. Nine years later another tragedy would claim the life of Cheryl's only son, Dionte. At the age of twelve he was brutally murdered in a drive-by shooting in Richmond, California. Life's offerings of misfortune to the Brown family finally ended with survival and hope for the future in the life of Cheryl's daughter, Shante. A beautiful young woman, who was raised by family, her mother's first cousin, Brenda (Hawkins) Cofer. Shante continues to be all the hope and dreams, maybe not, accomplished by her mother but certainly fulfilled by her daughter.

Ruth Mae Martin DOB: 7 March 1923

Ruth Mae Martin, oldest daughter of Willie and Lee Martin, was born in Ragley, Texas in Polk County. Ragley was a post office and timber-processing community northwest of Jefferson County. The community was probably named for the Ragley Lumber Company. She grew up in the somewhat isolated mill towns all over Polk, Trinity, Newton, Jefferson and Angelina Counties. As children Ruth and her brother Solomon and sister Ruby, attended church regularly and were also members of the "Woodsmen" a division of the Masons for children. During the Great Depression, she tells the story of how the farmers with plows dug up the ball park in Deweyville and made what they called a "Panic Garden", they grew vegetables for the sawmill workers, anybody could get food; white and black.

Ruth Mae Martin in Beaumont

She attended school when she could and helped her mother working as young as nine years old, washing dishes for a white lady in the sawmill town. She told us (my sister and brother), many stories of growing up and moving from town to town, when her Dad would leave one job for another. Being the oldest girl she had a tremendous responsibility in helping her mother with the younger children. She kept house, one of her many talents was painting. My sister, Brenda asked her one time, Mom why are you always painting something; walls, furniture, etc.? She answered, "I guess I like to paint, my mother always had me painting something." She told me of a summer job she had when she was only 14 years old. She worked for a wealthy white family in Beaumont. She was in charge of the children. She would travel in the summer with them to their summer home, in Denver, Colorado. Today she would be called a nanny. She told us of the many towns her family had lived: Volts, Hochel, Beaumont, Jasper, Deweyville, Trinity, New Willard, to name a few. She was promoted to 8th grade and the family moved from New Willard after Lee had left them again. They went to Beaumont where her mother struggled to support them and Aunt Leah came to help. Ruth and Solomon got jobs and when Ruby graduated she told her sister, "Now it's your turn to return to school, I'll stay home and help". Ruth had decided by then it was too late for her, so she never returned to school. She continued to work and help the family until she met the man she was to marry.

I found an original copy of my Mom's wedding invitation that stated, Mrs. Willie Watts request the honor of your presence at the marriage of her daughter Ruth to Mr. Warren Hawkins on Monday, the 29th of April nineteen hundred and forty-six. I asked my mother, "why didn't Mom Willie put **her** father's name (Lee) on the invitation, instead of her step-father? She didn't know but told me, "he never came to rehearsals, but he showed up. He tripped on my train, but he didn't fall, he just said, "oomph" and kept on stepping".

She married Warren and moved to start a new life in Northern California. Their first apartment was in North Oakland, California. Warren, just out of the Navy, was working for the Veterans Administration and Ruth, lonely in her new surroundings, would catch the trolley train in the evenings to meet him and they would ride home together. Ruth was not a very good cook, at first. She actually learned to cook from her husband and the cookbooks that he bought her. It didn't take long for them to start their family, their first child, a boy, did not survive, but on 5 January 1948, a daughter, Cynthia was born. Another daughter would soon follow on 18 January 1950, they named her Brenda. During this period Warren and Ruth, bought their first property in Berkeley and worked hard building a life for themselves and their girls, Warren returned to college and Ruth worked part-time to help out. Much to their surprise, nine years after Brenda's birth, they were expecting again, this time it would be a boy. Warren G. Hawkins, Jr. was born 23 August 1959, one week after his Dad's birthday. The now larger family would buy a home in

Richmond, California. Warren and Ruth would continue raising their kids, see them grow to adulthood and have children of their own. On 19 September 1984 Warren died while on an outing at the A's baseball game. Ruth was away at the time, in Beaumont, visiting her family there.

Warren G. Hawkins & Ruth Mae Martin, Beaumont, TX; Wedding Day April 29, 1946

Upon her return, I would be the one to pick her up at the airport, I remember seeing my mother never looking as venerable as she did, when she said, "it's just us now" . . . . . and that's how it has been. My strong mother, who is there for all of us and continues to be for her family, she continues to live life to the fullest, keeping herself busy with her church, her friends and family. For a school assignment in 2006, great-granddaughter, Jessica Murray sums it up like this: "I chose to interview my great-grandmother, Mrs. Ruth Hawkins because she is eighty-three years old and she has a lot of stories to tell me. She has lived through the 20s,30s,40s the 50s,60s,70s the 80s,90s and up to today 2006."

Excerpt of questions from Jessica's Interview with great-grandmother in 2006:

Q: What kind of environment did you grow up around as a teen?

A: My father was a sawmill worker and we traveled a lot, because when my Dad got mad about something on his job, he would quit and we would have to move to another sawmill town. We lived in a lot of towns.

The Hawkins Family, circa 1960s; l. to r. Ruth, Cynthia, Brenda, Warren Jr., & Warren Sr.

Q: As a teen did you have to attend church and why?

A: I attended church from birth because my mother and grandmother went to church all the time. On Sundays we were in church all day.

Q: What was your first job and paying wage?

A: Washing dishes for a lady, $1.00 a week in the 1930s.

Q When did you get your license and first car?

A: I did not get my license until I was grown and married. My first car was a Pontiac Tempest in the 60s.

Q: What chores did you have to do as you were maturing?

A: I helped my mother clean the house and helped care for my younger brothers. I did not like to cook. My sister did the cooking.

Q: Did you ever get into fights at school or any place else?

A: I would get into fights when I was younger because my sister and I were always defending our oldest brother, whose talk got him into trouble.

Q: Did you have a curfew and if so what time did you have to come in?

A: We could not be out after dark, unless it was church and we were always chaperoned. We did not have much idle time; we went to school and did our chores.

Q: Did you ever smoke or drink and why if you did?

A: We could not smoke or drink because of our religion and when I grew up I never wanted to.

Q: As a teen were a lot of things separated from blacks and whites?

A: I grew up when everything was separate, in the sawmill town there was a school for the whites and a school for the blacks. There were churches one for the whites and one for the blacks, we were called Negroes then.

Q: What was the hottest dance in high school?

A: Charleston and fox trot.

Thank you, the end.

Excerpts from Cynthia's Journal:

On one of my weekly visits to stay with my Mom, I began to keep a journal of our times together. I want to share a conversation we had about my mother's experience working when she was young.

Journal, Monday, October 14, 2008

We got up this morning; I started Mom's breakfast and had my tea. In a conversation with my Mom, she reveals to me a story about the white woman that she worked for in Beaumont, during the early 1940s, during World War II. Her name was Ms. Mildred. Mom worked as a Nanny. She cared for one of the woman's three children. She was directly responsible for washing that child's clothes and babysitting. She wore a uniform bought by her employer.

She said," I had a candy stripe uniform, the other maids wore white uniforms. I was about 18 years old at the time. I had a week to wash dishes, the cook's name was Cecilia, sometimes I did the grocery shopping for her and when I did, I would buy things for my mama that were

hard to get during the war; like sugar, eggs and milk. Ms. Cecilia was a neighbor of my mama's. Ms. Mildred was very wealthy and she had maids and workers for everything. The house was a mansion with a solarium, a library, it had an elevator in it and she had twin washing machines. There was a long table set up "outside" in the back of the house for the servants to eat their meals. Sometimes I brought my little brothers, they played in a room out of sight and Ms. Mildred didn't mind as long as she didn't see them. "Mom continues, "The mansion sat across the street from the family's many businesses; a drug store and other shops the family owned. When the family went out of town, the servants still had to work and the servants just took over the house. I enjoyed laying in their big king sized bed! The bartender would fix drinks for those who drank alcohol. The servants would party. We would sit at the "dining room" table for our meals!! "

Ruth (Martin) Hawkins and Warren Jr., Richmond, California

My Mom, the Activist

In the early 1960s my mother, Ruth Martin, was a card-carrying member of CORE (The Congress of Racial Equality); an organization founded by Mr. James Farmer, Jr., Mr. Farmer was recently re-introduced to the public via the movie, "The Great Debators". As a member of CORE, my mother attended meetings and participated in marches and picketing in the Northern California Bay Area. I am proud to point

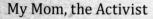

out that she also brought my sister and me along and we picketed grocery stores and businesses that at that time did not hire African Americans. I am very proud to note that my mother played a part in the Civil Rights Movement and contributed what she could to affect change. Discrimination didn't just occur in the south as some people at that time may have thought.

Ruby Lee Martin DOB: 15 August 1924

Ruby Lee or "Wee Wee" as the family would call her was the baby girl, youngest daughter of Lee and Willie was born in Hoshell, Texas. She grew up in the same sawmill towns as her brothers and sister. She graduated from Trinity High School. She met and married Raymond Mayfield 15 December 1944. She had one child, Ruby Jo Alice Mayfield, born on 4 November 1945. Ruby made a home for Raymond and Ruby Jo and at the same time worked for the Beaumont Independent School District. She was a Pastry Cook, today she probably would be called a Pastry Chef. Many of her nieces and nephews have had the pleasure of eating Aunt Ruby's cakes, pies, cinnamon rolls and anything she decides to cook.

Wonderful memories of visiting Beaumont in the summers for me, as a child, were waking up in the mornings to a big breakfast, with the family all around; my grandmother Willie, my parents, my uncles; Joe and Harry and my young cousins; Ruby and Jody. It was still the 1950s and many more cousins had yet to be born. Aunt Ruby and Uncle Raymond lived next door to Mama Willie and usually Aunt Ruby did a lot of the cooking for both homes, much as she did growing up, Aunt Ruby was the family's cook. A vivid memory for me; at breakfast after much begging, I was allowed a piece of the 4-layer chocolate cake, that Aunt Ruby had baked the night before. With that cake was a tall glass of orange juice, just delivered by the milkman. In those days, a milkman came in the mornings to deliver ice cold milk, juice, and other milk products. My love for "real butter" was developed there in my Grandmother's kitchen, where we ate hot grits, dripping in butter along with that wonderful Texas sausage.

Although, Ruth left home to live in California, it did not separate the sisterhood that they have always shared. I witnessed their closeness all my life. I recall the story my mother told of the three little children that were leaving a farmhouse that they had lived in briefly, in Jasper, Texas. Lee had left Willie and the children again, to find work at the next town. Willie was left to pack up and take the children to either of their parents as she so often did. Ruth says, "we would go stay with our grandma Carrie, Lee's mother sometimes, until Lee would come and get us. This particular time as they were leaving the farm house, they had to lift a heavy gate that had fallen and made it impossible to get out. They had to lift the gate; Solomon, Ruth and Ruby they all made it through, except their mama. The heavy gate fell on her and those three little children looked horrified as their mother struggled to lift the gate off her body. Those three used all their combined weight and lifted the gate to free their mother. Solomon was about 5-yrs; Ruth 3-yrs and little Ruby, just a baby at 2 yrs. old. Ruth says, "Their mother, Willie had a scar on her left shoulder and arm for the rest of her life". The bond that they share as sisters has always been an example for me and my sister. In the past friends and family kept in contact by writing letters, it was our ancestors method of email. Here are some examples of their correspondence.

In a letter, written to Ruby from Ruth's fiancé Warren *(Ruth did not like to write)*, who was away in the Navy during WWII; dated 20 June 1944 from Portsmouth, Virginia he writes: *"I've been busy, hardly had time to do anything. By the way a friend of mine is going to write to you."* Warren writes some in shorthand, in an effort to help Ruby practice her secretarial shorthand skills. He ends his attempt at matchmaking by saying, *"Well take it easy and answer soon with all the news."* Signed, Warren

In a letter from Ruby to Ruth, dated 22 November 1962, she writes:*"My Dear Sister, I received your letter and was glad to hear from you. We are all well, and hope you all are the same."* She continues to write about what is going on with family, the church and life's trials. She ends the letter with: *"Your Sister Ruby—P.S. Even though things are not like we want them to be, but we still have a lot to be thankful for."*

Aunt Ruby retired from the school district after 30 years of employment. She never left her mother, living next door to her during her married life and continuing to be her mother's companion and main caregiver until her death in 1997. She presently keeps herself busy with her involvement with her church and has been very instrumental in providing back-up to my mother's memory. What my mother may not remember, Aunt Ruby does. She has been helping with this genealogical project since 2006.

Ruby Jo Alice Mayfield, only child of Ruby Lee Martin and Raymond Mayfield, grew up in Beaumont, Texas. Upon graduation from high school she came to California to attend college. She lived with her Aunt Ruth and when she met and married Jimmie Bell, a soldier serving in the U.S. Army during the Vietnam War, she moved to San Francisco, her husband's home.

She continues to live and work in San Francisco. Ruby is employed as an Elementary Advisor/Community Relations Specialist, with the S.F. school district for the past 38 years. She has two sons, Jimmie Jr., and Todd and two grandchildren.; Jimmie III and LaTasha Bell.

Joe Perry Gregory DOB: 28 March 1934

In His Words (interview with Cynthia):

I was born in Lufkin, Texas, Angelina County at my grandmother's house, on 28 March 1934.

Important relatives to me at that time, was my Mama, my brothers and sisters and my grandparents; Grandma Alice and Grandpa Joe, my mother's parents and my Grandma Carrie . . . . . . Carrie West, my Dad's mother.

All my schools I attended in Beaumont; Martin Elementary, Pipkin Elementary. That was in the early 1940s. After elementary school I

went to Charleton Pollard. We moved around a lot and I went to the schools in the district where we lived. We lived on Peacock, they changed the name to Virgil, we moved to Caldwell, that's when I went to Pipkin and I know exactly when we moved on Caldwell, it was on the Sunday the Japanese bombed Pearl Harbor, 7 December 1941, we moved that weekend. I went to Pipkin for about four years, after that we moved to the south end house, Finis Street, I was in high school by then.

After high school I came and stayed with y'all in California, I went to Contra Costa College for a couple of years and I used to take care of you (Cynthia) and Brenda. We went to church and I would take you and your mother to church. After that I came home and got drafted into the Army. I stayed in the Army from 1957 to 1959 and then I got out in 1959, then went back and stayed another year. The summer of 1961 I got out again, I had something like a nine, ten year obligation. They called it inactive, but subject to recall. I got called back in during the Berlin Crisis.

On 1 October 1954, my first child was born, her mother named her Gwendolyn, but my mama (Willie) renamed her JoHelen and everybody calls her Jody. Gwendolyn's mother's name is Deloris Broussard.

I was twenty-five years old when I married Mary Jane McCleon. We were married in Orange, Texas on 22 June 1959. Oldest son of Willie Ruth and Perry Louis Gregory, Joe had a strong work ethic, at a young age he sold watermelons to earn money. According to sister Ruth, "he got the watermelons from mama's employer and sold them from the employer's parking lot, he was about seven or eight years old". In the 1960s, Joe began working for the Graham and McNicholas families, as a butler/chauffer, he continues to work for them, now having served three generations of the families. On 27 May 1964 Joe and Mary welcomed their first son, Jonathan. A second son, Timothy was born on 20 December 1965 and on 26 June 1970, their third and last child, a son was born, Perry Naaman.

In 1973, Joe began working for the Beaumont Independent School District as a carpenter. He would retire from BISD, twenty-six years later as Supervisor of Grounds and Maintenance for the entire school district. Joe has been a life-long member of the Church of the Living God, where he faithfully serves as Chairman of the Trustee Board and the Superintendent of Sunday School.

Joe and Mary continue to live a life surrounded by their children and grandchildren. Both are retired, but they both continue to work at different projects, for family and the community. Most recently, they celebrated their 50th Wedding Anniversary, with family and friends at the Country Club in Beaumont.

Cynthia's Memories of her Uncle Joe:

"My mother's younger brother, Joe came to live with us in the early 1950s. I was about seven or eight years old. We lived in Berkeley, California. I recall a neighbor that lived down the street, we called her Sister Lester, she was an old friend of our grandmother, who had moved from Beaumont to California. She had all these daughters, about four or five of them. They were always after Uncle Joe; coming around and looking for him, wanting him to give them a ride somewhere, any excuse to be with him. It was funny to watch him hiding and trying to avoid them, he just wasn't interested. He attended community college during his stay with us and one foggy morning, the fog was real thick in the mornings. Joe was on his way to school, he was driving across the railroad tracks, down the street from our house. Well, Uncle Joe heard the train whistling coming down the tracks and not knowing how close the train was, he jumped out of my Daddy's car and left it on the tracks. The train hit the car with some damage, but Uncle Joe was safe. The family laughed and joked about that incident for a long time."

"Uncle Joe has a unique sense of humor, and he likes to cook. During his stay with us my Dad would assign duties to everyone in the household and Uncle Joe's day to cook was on Friday, sometimes we had fish on Fridays. He would fry or bake this elaborate fish dish and make potato salad with these very creative garnishes and decorations. I always looked forward to his concoctions; they almost looked to good to eat. He was a big fan of the Negro Baseball Leagues and Jackie Robinson was one of his favorite players and also Satchel Paige, the famous Negro Leagues pitcher. Uncle Joe stayed with us for a couple of years, and then he returned to Beaumont and went into the Army."

"Most recently (2010), I was grateful for the time I got to spend with Uncle Joe and Aunt Mary. We went on a "road trip" to Lufkin, just for me to do research and meet some folks in Lufkin."

Harry Lewis Gregory DOB: 8 August 1936

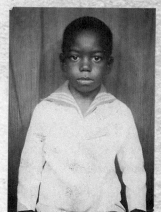

Harry Lewis Gregory was born in Trinity, Texas, the youngest son of Willie and Perry Gregory. Harry grew up in Beaumont, the family left Trinity when Harry was a baby. As he became school age, he would spend summers with various relatives. Willie worked and the older children worked so Harry would stay with others when he was on school vacation. Some summers he would travel by bus to the town of Kountze, where he spend the summer with his step-dad, Lee Martin. Lee called him, "little buddy".

Harry was truly the Mama's boy and everybody knew it. He was a free spirit and very sociable. When we visited Texas in the summer, Uncle Harry was always out somewhere, he was still a teenager when I met him for the first time.

Harry continued his schooling and graduated from Charleton Pollard High School. Shortly after graduating he married Marie Richard on 8 November 1958. Harry and Marie have three children; Harry Jr., born 15 November 1961, Mark, born 31 August 1963 and their only daughter; Annette was born on 2 August 1974.

Harry worked for the 7-Up Company, he started working for 7-Up right out of high school and worked for them serving 46 years as a driver/delivery man. "I remember my uncle working for the 7-UP Beverage Company, he would show up at Mama Willie's at lunchtime in that big old truck", says Cynthia. Aunt Marie worked for the Beaumont Independent School District as a bus driver, retiring after 25 years.

Harry, like all his brothers and sisters before him, is a life-long member of the Church of the Living God. The Uncle Harry that I know today is one of the kindest people around. He is very active in his church. He serves as a member of COTLG-Concord; fulfilling the duties of Chairman of

Trustees and as Sunday School Superintendent, and he is also a singer, singing in the Men's Chorus. I was glad I had the opportunity to hear him sing at his church and hear him singing "country songs" in his truck, during a visit in November 2006.

A Memory of Uncle Harry: "Another one of my mother's stories was about Uncle Harry. When we were growing up we were told many stories about her and her brothers and sister, about their lives growing up. She also told us about a story that "her"mother would read to Uncle Harry, when he was a little boy. It was The Story of Epinundous,(pronounced eppa-nun-dous), about a little boy who literally always did what he was told, somehow he always got it wrong. For instance, one day Epinundous' mother had baked some pies and set them out on the porch to cool. She instructed Epinundous to "step over" the pies. Well, Epinundous stepped "in" the pies.

The story always repeated, "But he was a good little boy and always did what he was told". This story was always funny to us and when we didn't follow instructions, our mother would say, "you are just like Epinundous". Another example of the strong family bond experienced first hand for me was when Uncle Harry put aside his fear of flying and he got on a plane with his brother Joe and sister Ruby, to attend the funeral of his sister Ruth's husband in 1984. His first visit to the state of California helped to brighten the saddest day of my life and I will be forever grateful.

Harry and Marie Gregory
Beaumont, Texas, November 2009.

Annette (Gregory) Rodgers with Kyra & Kaleb.

Harry Gregory Jr. & Mark Gregory

Chapter 7

Harry Smith's Children

Corrine Smith—DOB: 15 Jul 1934 – DOD: 4 February 2003

Corrine, one of twin girls, was born to Harry and Mary Ella (Saddler) Smith in Camden, Texas. The twins were the first born children for Harry and Mary Ella. Corrine, known to family as "Tea", grew up in and attended schools in the sawmill towns of Camden and others in East Texas, until the family moved to Lufkin to live with Grandma Alice. Corrine grew up and moved to New Mexico, where she met and married Willie Brown Finley, who served in the military. As a military wife, she traveled around the country with her husband. They settled in Milwaukee, Wisconsin. Corrine had four children; a son Willie Jr., and three daughters; Alice, Terry and Lourynn. Corrine was hospitalized and after a long illness passed away on Tuesday, February 4, 2003. She is buried at the Veteran's Memorial Cemetery, in Union Grove, Wisconsin.

Marine Smith—DOB: 15 July 1934

Spouse: Edmond Minor

Marine Smith, the oldest daughter along with her twin, Corrine, is called "Sister" by all family members who know her. She was born in Camden, a large sawmill town in Polk County. She grew up attending schools in Camden and later Carver and Dunbar schools in Lufkin, Texas. Along with her parents, brothers and sister, she came to live in Lufkin, when her parents decided to move, after the death of Grandpa Joe.

Marine was very active in school, as a majorette and she played saxophone in the school band. She married her high school sweetheart and shortly after began her family. She has seven children,

Marine and Edmond Minor, Wedding Day 13 July 2001

two of them, a son and a daughter, are now deceased. Over the years she has worked to provide and care for her growing children after her first marriages didn't work out.

In her own words, "I got good jobs and worked hard to buy my home to be able to clothe and feed my kids, I attended their school activities and I didn't smoke or drink".

She retired from work as a dietician and cook for Ramanor Cafeteria. Her latest job has been as foster mother, providing care for children in need of a good and loving home.

In 2001 she married Edmond Minor and resides in Houston, Texas. She enjoys traveling, spending time with her children and grandchildren and keeping in contact with her brothers, sister Dorothy and other family members.(*Sadly Edmond passed away in December 2012.)*

Marine's Children are:

Larry Donnell Smith, DOB April 1951; Mary Parks, DOB October 1952; Jerry Earl Parks, DOB February 1954; Jefferey Wheeler, DOB June 1955 – DOD May 1990; Jerald Wheeler Jr., DOB June 1956; Lily Faye Wheeler,DOB July 1957 – DOD December 2001.

A.J. Smith – DOB: 16 April 1936

Parents: Harry Smith, Mary Ella Saddler

Spouse (No information available)

A.J. Smith, oldest son of Harry and Mary Ella, was born in Camden, Polk County, Texas. He left home at a young age and traveled to Seattle, Washington, where he resides. He is the father of a daughter named Patty. According to sister Marine, "A.J. is retired and enjoys hanging out at Starbucks, watching the lovely ladies go by". A.J. is named for his grandfather Joe and grandmother Alice.

L.C. Smith – DOB: 5 September 1937

Parents: Harry Smith, Mary Ella Saddler

Spouse: Vivan Craddock

L.C. Smith, was also born in Camden, starting his young life in the sawmill town, like many of his relatives. He was adventurous, not content to live under the strict rule of his father and mother. He tells his story in an interview recorded by me on 3 February 2010.

Cynthia: Starting with a review of our previous conversation, L.C. your sons' names are:

L.C.: Stanley Smith, the oldest lives in Phoenix, Arizona, he has eight children. My 2nd son's name is Marcus, he lives in Brownwood with me and his mother.

L.C.: I am a retired heavy equipment operator and I am a minister. I did not serve in the military. They told me I was a lover, they wants fighters (laughs).

L.C.: I was about six years old when we moved to Lufkin, just getting ready to go to school.

Cynthia: Asks about L.C.'s older sister, Corrine?

"I don't know how old Corrine was when she left home. I wasn't there, cause I was long gone, I wasn't even there when she got married. I left home when I was about twelve years, I went to Midland (Texas), I took care of myself, got odd jobs, farm labor, etc., I went around Arizona, then back to Midland, then back to Arizona. I lived in Los Angeles for about two years, working wherever I could. I left Los Angeles and went back to Phoenix, then to Idaho and Las Vegas and back to Phoenix, then to Odessa, Texas."

Cynthia: Did you meet your wife in Arizona?

L.C. Smith with wife Vivan Craddock.

L.C.: You bet I did and her home was in Mt. Pleasant, Texas. Yes, her home was in Texas too, but we met in Arizona. Yeh, first love, at first sight. What do you call, love at first sight, that's what it was. I told a preacher friend of mine, well, now he's a preacher. I said, "there's my wife, and I married her". "Yes sir.""Don't know what happened to Grandma's things, Aunt Leah probably had them, but that woman that lived next door to Leah and Melvin, that took care of her (Leah) before she died. Grandma had some interesting photos, don't know what happened. I wanted to see Uncle Melvin, when I came back, but they told me that woman wasn't gonna let nobody see him. She was trying to get him to sign over everything to her, before he died. I never got to see him, she wouldn't let me come in. She ended up with the house. Uncle Melvin drank a lot, she got in there and tricked him into signing. Melvin didn't have any kids, if he had kids, they didn't show up, nobody knew it."

Stanley & Shiki Smith with Family,
Phoenix, Arizona

"My church is in Coleman, Texas, been pastoring for 26 years. Not many members, I know when somebody is not there. But they coming back, when things are bad, Black folks come to church. God Bless." *(Ed. Note L.C. lost his beloved wife Vivan in November 2012 after a long illness.)*

L.C.'s Children and Grandchildren:

Stanley Smith – DOB: February 1959

Parents: L.C. Smith, Susie Dunbar; Spouse Shiki Taylor

Childrens' names: Jada, Jonie, Brianna, Aubrie, Maya,

Stanella, Naya,

Westley, London, Paris

Marcus Isaiah Smith – DOB: January 1992

Parents: L.C. Smith, Vivan Craddock

Mary Ella Barnes DOB: abt. 1957 (no photo available)

Parents: L.C. Smith, Vivan Craddock

Marcus Isaiah Smith, Brownwood, Texas

Wiley Smith

DOB: April 1943

The youngest son of Harry Smith and Mary Ella Saddler, resides in Lufkin, Texas. The following information was confirmed by him at a prior interview. All other attempts to contact failed.

Spouse name, Delores Morris; daughters, Jacqueline Michelle Smith and Lisa Dianne Smith.

Brothers and sister; L.C., Marine and Wiley Smith in Lufkin, Texas.

My Epilogue

My deep appreciation for history has always drawn me to do research and read about the past. I <u>needed</u> to write this book, and along the way try to include some of our family's history. I hope that you have read this collection and gotten acquainted with the folks who started this family, learning their names, where they lived and a little about how they lived. They were ordinary people, who survived under extraordinary circumstances. It is important for our children to know that the rights and freedoms that we enjoy did not come easily and many rights that we have earned are being subjected to reversal or elimination to this day.

Our family's story begins in the state of Texas and our history begins just before slavery ends. Texas slaves were informed of their freedom on June 19, 1865, at the end of the Civil War but the Emancipation Proclamation had been issued in January 1863. It took Texas a couple of years to accept and along with the 13th Amendment in 1865 ,acknowledge that our people were free; once that was realized, I believe, that on the very next day white folks started working to put laws in place to remind all black folks of the perils of believing that they were free and equal. These were called **Black Codes** and what would eventually become **Jim Crow** Laws.

Here's a brief timeline of the period before slavery and up to the Civil Rights Era:

1619-1863 – Most blacks in the United States were enslaved by white people, although there were free blacks living in the United States before and during slavery.

1861 – The Civil War begins in the United States.

1863 – Emancipation Proclamation legally frees all slaves in the Confederacy, including Texas.

1865 – The 13th amendment passes outlawing slavery.

1866 – The all white legislatures in the former confederate states pass "Black Codes" which restricts freedom for African Americans thereby re-enslaving them.

1866 – The 1st Civil Rights Act passes Congress granting citizenship on African Americans.

1925 – Required racially segregated schools.

1940s – Separate seating on all buses.

1950s – Public accommodations; separate facilities required for Blacks and Whites:

Parks, restrooms and drinking fountains.

1951 – Poll tax required paying to vote

1951 – Unlawful for persons of Caucasian blood to marry persons of African blood; penalty is two to five years imprisonment.

1954 – Brown v. Board of Education abolished the separate but equal policy of segregated schools.

1958 – In Texas, no child is compelled to attend schools that are racially mixed. No desegregation unless approved by election. The Governor may close schools where troops used on federal authority.

This is by no means the only laws that were passed, a total of twenty-seven Jim Crow laws were passed in Texas alone, from 1866 to 1958.

The stories of history and the stories of our family, coincide with each other. I grew up after World War II, during the 1950s and up to the 1960s and the Civil Rights Era. My grandparents and parents lived during the different eras that were also significant periods of history. Our grandparents didn't tell their stories of slavery and oppression to their children and consequently our parents didn't tell my sister and me, or our brother, about the Jim Crow south. I learned about the Jim Crow south during a summer vacation in 1957. The very young years, for my sister and I, took place from 1948 to the early 1950s. The president of the United States was a fellow named Dwight Eisenhower, a retired army general from World War II; actually he was a WWII hero. The times were not the greatest for people of color. Inequality was rampant, especially in the southern states of America. For me growing up in Berkeley during the 1950s life was idyllic. We didn't know about the rest of the country. As far as we knew, we were equal. We grew up on a beautiful tree lined street with neighbors from various ethnic groups, some were first or second generation immigrants to this country, everyone, I believed, was focused on educating and raising their families.

For my actual experience with Jim Crow and lunch counters and eating out, please read on. My younger sister was about 6 years old and I was about 8 or 9 years old. We customarily met our mother for lunch downtown about once a week or so. Our mother worked as a part-time housekeeper and in those days kids could walk around or catch buses at our ages freely without any worry. We would catch the bus downtown and meet our mother at Woolworths "5 and Dime" Store, a "5 and Dime" was a variety store; it sold hardware, general dry goods and novelty items, not groceries. Anyway these "5 and Dime" stores also had lunch counters. It was a treat for us; our mom would meet us after she got off work. We sat at the counter and had a favorite at the time, club sandwiches with french fries, a coca cola and maybe a slice of chocolate cake. Then with a $1.00, yes one dollar in hand, we would shop, buying little items; doll clothes or penny candy. This was our future training for shopping with our mother. We all love to shop!

My mom (Ruth) with neighbor Laura Bennette on our beautiful street in Berkeley.

"Fast forward" to the summer of 1957 we traveled to visit our relatives in Texas, unaware, that our Dad drove all day and we slept in the car at night, because we couldn't stay in motels along the way. My sister and I didn't realize, we were just kids on a rode trip, it was fun for us. We arrive in Texas; we are visiting with our relatives. One bright morning we catch the bus to go downtown with our cousin Ruby Jo. We pay our fare and I sit down on the bench right behind the driver as I was accustomed to doing. Ruby yells as she walks towards the back of the bus, "get up, you can't sit there". I obediently get up; she's my older cousin, so I don't give her any problems. In my defense, in retrospect, I didn't notice any signs. Anyway, I didn't question why I had to get up; I just thought she wanted me to sit in the back with her and my sister. Well, we get downtown, in those days it's not the mall. Downtown is the strip, with blocks of stores, shoe shops, department stores, banks and other businesses. This was downtown, where everybody shopped. We find Woolworths and the lunch counter, I order a snow cone, it's Texas in the summer, and it's hot. I get my snow cone and I sit down on one of the stools at the counter, ok, there's Ruby yelling at me again, to "get up", I can't sit there. I must have been a dumb kid, because I just got up and we browsed around a little and left the store. I don't remember asking why? Why did I have to get up, why couldn't I sit at Woolworths. I didn't know and our parents didn't tell us. We were sheltered from the truth. Our parents thought they were protecting us. It would be a few years before I understood what my parents tried to protect my sister and me from. Years later, when we marched and held picket signs protesting unfair hiring practices of a major grocery store chain, I understood why we had to participate in that display of demanding equal rights in the 60s. I am proud. That's progress, even if at the time, some white boys drove by spitting at us from their car and throwing pennies at us. There were many who endured worse indignities including death, for speaking and protesting. I hope the stories in this book will instill a pride in my children and grandchildren with a desire to accomplish and achieve in life what our forefathers couldn't.

There will always be challenges to our lives as black folks. It is important to stay educated and informed. Laws may change but most change is not allowed without a vote. You may have to fight to protect your rights by voting and taking an active role in your communities, schools and government.

The year 2013 brought the Trayvon Martin murder by George Zimmerman and subsequent trial and verdict to remind us of the realities of living in the United States as a black person. With the current tide of racial inequality, and the gun violence, those of us with a memory of similar times will remember, Emmett Till, in the 1950s. In 2009 for us in the Northern California Bay Area, the Oscar Grant III tragedy, has been brought back with the release of the movie (Fruitvale Station) depicting that unfair, unfortunate occurrence of an act taking yet another young black man's life, so unnecessarily.

Cynthia with four of her grandsons l. to r. Derrick, Justin, Joseph and Dahryl.

There are far too many names to remember, even if we could remember the names, that's would not change what is continuing to happen to our young men. What is important to me is the way these young men are viewed or looked at. My young men, my sons and grandsons, nephews, my brother what I see would never be someone to shoot and kill. They are NOT Thugs! My younger brother who is not a boy, he is a grown man. He told me of an incident that occurred during his working environment. He works for a public utility company and is routinely called to the homes of customers for repair work. He told me of reporting to a particular home and upon arriving and knocking at the door; he is informed that there must be a mistake, no one called for service. Well, he kindly left but he had the opportunity to overhear the conversation in regards to his visit. The company was told that my brother looked like a bum. He wore his normal work attire with identifying badge, hat, shirt, and jacket, whatever. So, what made him look like a bum? I hear the pain in my brother's voice when he tells me of this incident. What I see is the kind sensitive little brother that I grew up with, who matured into a strong, caring, nurturing father to his son and grandson. What that customer saw didn't exist, except in her small mind.

My grandsons; what I see is one little boy that followed me around in the kitchen when he was just a small fellow. He is now a chef and loves his work. One of my other little fellows started his own small business, cutting lawns and had built up quite a clientele; he was to continue college courses in horticulture. He was riding in a car with friends and someone was trying to shoot someone in the car; the bullet grazed his head, he has recovered from his wound. He gave up horticulture, I don't know why. Another one of my fellows entertains the family with his standup comedy routine and he was once a tap dancer, he loved acting in school plays; he is trying to cope with "Post Traumatic Stress Syndrome", since having a gun held to his head at a party, for no apparent reason. Another one of my guys was on the honor roll in elementary and middle school; he has always gone his own way, never causing trouble for anyone. One day he was walking down the street, someone starting shooting at him, he narrowly got away with a minor wound to his leg. My boys, the sons of my daughters are like so many young black men, just trying to survive. They have plenty to contend with in their own environments without the added jeopardy of being singled out to be "shot while being black", or wearing a hoodie, or wearing braids or locks, whatever excuse it is for simply being brown or black. My little boys AND girls, you are all very precious to me. We are all the children of Marqurette – "Cut From the Same Cloth", you are here because SHE Survived.

The End

Bibliography

Baker, R. S. (1983). *Sawdust Empire, The Texas Lumber Industry 1830-1940.* Austin, Texas: Texas A&M University Press.

Barr, A. (1973, 1995). *Black Texans, A History of African Americans in Texas, 1528-1995.* Austin, Texas: Jenkins Book Publishing Co., University of Oklahoma Press.

Sitton, Thad & Conrad, James H., (1998), *Nameless Towns, Texas Sawmill Communities 1880-1942*, University of Texas Press, Austin

AuthorHouse™ LLC
1663 Liberty Drive
Bloomington, IN 47403
www.authorhouse.com
Phone: 1-800-839-8640

Published by AuthorHouse 01/24/2014

ISBN: 978-1-4918-4249-2 (sc)
      978-1-4918-4262-1 (e)

Library of Congress Control Number: 2013923308

Any people depicted in stock imagery provided by Thinkstock are models,
and such images are being used for illustrative purposes only.
Certain stock imagery © Thinkstock.

This book is printed on acid-free paper.

Because of the dynamic nature of the Internet, any web addresses or links contained in this book may have changed
since publication and may no longer be valid. The views expressed in this work are solely those of the author and do
not necessarily reflect the views of the publisher, and the publisher hereby disclaims any responsibility for them.

author**HOUSE**®

"Cut *from* the same cloth"

A Collection of Smith Family Stories 1841 - 2006

C. A. HAWKINS